L' impossi preneurs

A Hopeful Journey
Through Tomorrow

Gregory J. Olson

DEDICATION

This book is especially dedicated to my father, James Eugene Olson. This man crafted bumpers for his 39 Ford pickup using Mustang bumpers. He also reshaped a telephone company utility box to fit on the truck bed. These are seemingly impossible tasks for those lacking skills or worse, the imagination to envision the possibilities and begin such a project. Now retired, my father has moved his imagination from customizing cars to writing. If you enjoy a good mystery please check out his books: *The Deadly Souvenir; The Switch;* and *A Death in Mahler County.*

This book is also dedicated to Darryl Bills whom I worked with at the Boeing Wind Tunnel. It was he who taught me to use a jeweler's lathe, water welder, and various other tools of the trade in crafting models planes to fly in the wind tunnel. But, most of all he taught me that if you can see it in your mind's eye, then you can surely build it.

CONTENTS

"The difficult is done at once; the impossible takes a little longer."

Anthony Trollope
British novelist and
postal worker occasionally
inspired by the
contents of lost letters
(1815–1882)

"I believe things cannot make themselves impossible"

Stephen William Hawking
Theoretical physicist,
cosmologist, author
(born 8 January 1942)

ACKNOWLEDGMENTS

Thank you to my friends, family, Olympic Club Seattle colleagues, and others who interacted with me.

Whether sharing ideas directly or saying something that sparked my imagination, I appreciate your participation in this project and for meeting me in my own wheel of life on this little planet we share.

Special thanks to Lika who shared her imaginative ideas as well as served as a sounding board for the "impossibilities" in this book.

And, thank you to those who purchased my first book, *The Experience Design Blueprint*. Your support has encouraged my continued exploration on this writer's journey.

Much appreciation to my editors Lisa Baker, James Olson, and Lika Hongthong who helped me create a better book so you could have a better reading experience.

Trademark disclaimer: any likeness to products or services, real or imagined, is purely coincidental. Chock it up to the collective unconscious and popular culture. Any brands or links provided are information and not an endorsement. This is especially true of personal teleporter technology.

INTRODUCTION

Imagination is a powerful force. It can help us to envision something better than the current state of things. This is easily represented by looking at a situation where a person is disadvantaged. Dwell on that for a moment, a disadvantaged person.

No doubt, you've already added some context to the situation. Perhaps when you thought of disadvantaged you thought of a person with a physical impairment or someone who is financially distressed. Maybe they don't have meaningful employment or have an addiction. There are a multitude of disadvantages that could be considered.

However, what you specifically thought of was likely based on your own personal experience. Whether it was something that happened to you directly or you were merely an observer, your brain built a connection between what you read here and what you already knew. See, your imagination is a powerful force.

Connecting what you hear to your own experience isn't the most interesting thing about your imagination though. When confronted with a situation, your imagination goes to work crafting a solution, finding a better way. When you think of the plight of disadvantaged people, your mind automatically begins solution finding. Mobility problem? Of course, that person needs a wheelchair or crutches.

But, disadvantaged comes in many forms. And, what may have been a disadvantage in the past is no longer necessarily relevant today. Consider hunters and gatherers who imagined and then built weapons and carry systems. Most of us don't worry about such things in modern life. Instead we worry that the grocery store checkout line might be too long and more recently that we'll be forced to use the self-service checkout. It is, of course, relative though. In an interview with Mariam Dao Gabala, former West Africa regional manager for social investor Oikocredit International, she shared that today 100's of millions of people in eight West Africa countries are being fed using 15th century farming methods.

No matter our personal plight or good fortune, we all share a common humanity and a shrinking planet. So, it is a good thing that our imagination can be a powerful force toward benefiting all of us. A common refrain today that was popularized with President Franklin Delano Roosevelt is, "We all do better when we all do better."

When our imaginations are aligned it can be a force for change. When enough people desire improvements, then new conversations arise. And, when there are enough of these new conversations, it turns out change may already be afoot. If you are familiar with the terms emergence or crowd intelligence you already know this phenomenon. If you are not familiar you might consider scheduling a side trip to a great Radiolab podcast on the subject.[1]

A study of most any period of history will reveal a human spirit that doesn't stand still for very long. Whether it is cultural, technological, social, spiritual, or some other type of change, humans are usually running from the current state and seeking what's next.

Working in concert to make things better through

design makes humans unique compared to other animals in the Animal Kingdom. Polar bears might be negatively affected by climate change, but their imaginations are ill equipped to envision, discuss, design, and implement solutions.

Today, most people accept climate change, that the earth is round and revolves around the sun, and that germs cause disease. But, this wasn't always the case. People were afraid to embrace ideas that were different for fear that they, like many of the proponents of the new, would be imprisoned, ostracized, banished, or worse, killed.

Today, fortunately, it is safe to use your imagination. It is also safe to share those dreams and ideas without fear of such persecution (at least in the civilized world). Like travel, good meals, and other indulgences, dreams are best shared with others. So, I offer you this collection of possibilities that have yet to materialize.

It is my hope that ideas shared in this book will capture the imagination of others and some ideas will begin to take shape. Some of these ideas may look familiar. Some may sound a bit strange. Some may be good and others may not be. Time will ultimately be the judge and the jurors will likely be those yet to be born.

Before we dive into some future possibilities let us first ask the question, who would devote their time and energy toward making the possible future unfold? The likely doers of what's next will be entrepreneurs. But, as we'll discover in the next chapter, that label of entrepreneurs is not quite descriptive enough.

1 FLAVORS OF ENTREPRENEURSHIP

I believe entrepreneurship is a bit like dessert. There are many different types and the flavor varies, depending upon whom you ask. If I asked you, would you like some dessert? You'd likely respond, "What are you serving?" And, if I offered you a fruit plate versus cake, your answer might be different.

Like dessert, there are many versions of entrepreneurship and some people find some versions more to their taste than others.

Before I share the various flavors of entrepreneurship, let's make sure we start with the same basic understanding.

The classic definition of an entrepreneur is a person who starts a business and is willing to risk loss in order to make money.

A bit of history is in order. The term entrepreneur is Old French, from entreprendre (pronounced ahn tra pron) and means to undertake (begin or initiate).

Though people have been starting things since people have been around, the term entrepreneur wasn't actually used until 1723.

Credit for coining the term entrepreneur goes to Irish-

French economist Richard Cantillon who defined it first in a book written in 1730, and is considered the first complete treatise on economics. In his book, Cantillon conceives of the notion of the entrepreneur as a risk-bearer.

Like many words the meaning shifts to suit the time. Today the term entrepreneur implies qualities of leadership, initiative and innovation in business. But that is again like calling tiramisu and a fruit plate simply dessert. I think a bit more description is needed.

So, let's talk about the many flavors of entrepreneurs. You might recognize yourself in one of the types, either from your past, present, or your future. Or, you could very well see your neighbor, mother, uncle, daughter, colleague or classmate.

Entrepreneur – this is the traditional risk taker who sees the path they are forging as less risky than working for somebody else doing something that isn't interesting, isn't rewarding, or may conflict with their values.

Intrapreneur – this is an employee entrepreneur who has many of the risk elements of an entrepreneur, but is insulated from the brutal reality of having to manufacture their own paycheck. I once had the luxury of starting a business within a mature business and didn't have to worry about making money. That was a nice luxury compared to when I started a software company and had to worry about creating a paycheck for myself and for my employees.

Most people you've worked with in your past are probably not intrapreneurs. They are another type.

Loyalpreneur – these are employees dedicated to carrying out the orders of those they work for in exchange for a paycheck. In essence, trading hours for dollars.

Solopreneur – this is an entrepreneur acting in isolation without the support of an organization. Jay Sorenson, the inventor of the Java Jacket coffee sleeve, is a good example. He started alone solving a nagging problem. While taking his daughter to school, Jay dropped a cup of hot coffee in his lap that he received from a local coffee drive-thru. The paper cup was too hot. That got him thinking there must be a better way. The obvious solution to Jay was an insulated sleeve. What started as a small business selling product from the back of a car is now a thriving family business.[1]

Multipreneur – these are entrepreneurs who pursue multiple interests at the same time. Multipreneurs are sometimes confused with ...

Serial Entrepreneur – these are difference than Multipreneurs in that serial entrepreneurs usually pursue one idea at a time.

Don't recognize yourself or someone you know in one of these type of entrepreneurs yet? Well, read on.

Wannapreneur – these wishful people want to start something but don't yet know what. They might be lured by the glamour of high profile companies such as Google, Amazon, Dell, or Facebook. But they may lack a solid idea. They may be lying in wait for that great idea.

Socialpreneur – these special entrepreneurs are socially conscious individuals who create a business to remedy a problem in society, while still making a profit.

An example of a socialpreneur might be the person who improves the lives of families by turning an abandoned parking lot into a community garden.

Dreamapreneur – this entrepreneur dreams of pursuing a new passion, but really never commits to action.

It is simply more fun for these people to fantasize about the possibilities. Perhaps they lack a clear path forward, the conviction to start, or don't want to abandon the comfort of the easy chair. Dreamapreneurship is easy but not as rewarding as the real thing.

Elderpreneur – these are people who have decided to take their wealth of experience, network, and skills, then package them up into a credible story told with authority and conviction that might be lacking in younger entrepreneurs.

One such Elderpreneur is Harland David Sanders (Colonel Sanders) who in his earlier years was many of the other types of 'preneurs as well. At one point he started a company that made acetylene lights, but that venture flamed out when Delco introduced an electric lamp sold on credit.

The Colonel didn't franchise his first Kentucky Fried Chicken restaurant until 1952, at the age of 62. He pursued that concept in earnest until 1964 when the international expansion began to overwhelm him. He sold for $2M and then took a salaried position with the acquiring investment company and subsequently became the Kentucky Fried Chicken brand ambassador – the role we all know best.

Adventurepreneur – these workplace entrepreneurs work only to play. These folks might literally have a sign on their door, "Gone Fishing." I once worked with a young woman who job hopped to support her rock climbing addiction.

Addictipreneur – this person relentlessly pursues the next shiny new idea and then abandons it before the fledgling idea takes flight. So, the business never matures before the addictipreneur moves on to their next passion. It is hard to support this type of 'preneur.

Philanthropreneur – these people support other peoples' projects and ventures often times without concern for any payback. Philanthropreneurs sometime use crowdfunding platforms such as GoFundMe or Kickstarter.

I have a friend who is a single mother with a special needs child in a wheelchair. She needed a new (used van) with a wheelchair lift. Philanthropreneurs fully funded a campaign to buy her a new one. And the best thing is she didn't even create the campaign, her sister did, initially without her knowledge.

Luckypreneur – this is the fortunate person who has a job that allows them to make a big impact, make a good living, and make a difference in the world.

There you have it. Dessert has been served. You see, just like desserts, there are many types of entrepreneurs. I've shared more than a dozen. You might have thought of some of your own.

Whether you are tinkering in your garage or in your mind, you are likely a mix of these types of 'preneurs. No matter what form of entrepreneurship you might take or support I do believe that pursuing a passion with initiative is a valuable pursuit by itself. By doing so, you could manufacture your own luck, you might meet some very interesting people that enrich your life, and most of all you'll definitely not be bored.

And, if you're spurred to action, you might make the world a little better for people. Just like Jay did with the little Java Jacket that has now sold over four billion units and makes the hot beverage dessert in your cup a little safer to drink.

You might be thinking to yourself that something is missing. You might feel that you or the purveyors of the future belong in another category of entrepreneur, something that doesn't quite fit the labels and descriptions I've shared so far. You might be thinking that some ideas don't seem practical or are a little too advanced to even get started. If that is describing you then you would not be alone. You have much company in your very special category that is fixated on what appears to be fanciful or nonpractical today. That is the subject of the next chapter and the rest of this book.

2 THE IMPOSSIPRENEUR

Some people have a very valid reason to not get started on their ideas. They may have imagined something that isn't technically feasible using today's technology. Or, it might be that the idea isn't feasible from a business perspective. Even an idea that is technically feasible and viable as a business may encounter cultural or political barriers that impede its progress. People who propose ideas like this and face barriers that prevent their acceptance are **Impossipreneurs – L' impossi preneur.**

This isn't a new phenomena. Niccolò Machiavelli warned us similarly centuries ago.

"And it ought to be remembered that there is nothing more difficult to take in hand, more perilous to conduct, or more uncertain in its success, than to take the lead in the introduction of a new order of things.

Because the innovator has for enemies all those who have done well under the old conditions and lukewarm defenders in those who may do well under the new.

This coolness arises partly from fear of the opponents, who have the laws on their side, and partly from the incredulity of men, who do not readily believe in new things until they have had a long experience of them.

Thus it happens that whenever those who are hostile have the opportunity to attack they do it like partisans, whilst the others defend lukewarmly...."

Niccolò Machiavelli
Italian Diplomat, Political Philosopher,
Musician, Poet,
and Playwright
(1469–1527)

Eventually though, great ideas tear down or circumvent the barriers that oppose them. It's hard to resist an idea whose time has come. The world changes and the grand or even ludicrous visions of one epoch actually become commonplace in another.

Sometimes change is promulgated through the persistence of a visionary. In the case of the world's first publicly owned park, that visionary person was Ferdinand V. Hayden. After a couple of exploratory expeditions over a decade, Hayden proposed setting aside a 2,219,789 acre swath of land in Wyoming, Idaho, and Montana, comprising lakes, canyons, rivers and mountain ranges as a pleasure ground for the benefit and enjoyment of the people.[1]

It is worth mentioning that he wasn't acting alone. He wasn't the only impossipreneur in this case. The proposition was essentially the same as those earlier suggestions advanced by Thomas F. Meagher (1865), David E. Folsom (1869), and Cornelius Hedges (1870), but in this case it helped to shape a course of action which accomplished the objective.[2]

The bill to create the first national park, Yellowstone, was established by the U.S. Congress and signed into law by U.S. President Ulysses S. Grant. on March 1, 1872. This was thought to be a radical idea at the time.

Thankfully, the radical idea became less so and spread to eventually include actions of many other presidents and to the creation of the National Parks Service whose mission is to preserve the natural and cultural resources of the nation for the enjoyment, education, and inspiration of current and future generations.

Now, over 275 million annual visitors enjoy more than 400 such places.[3] It is worth noting that these places are owned by the public, not aristocrats, a monarch or captains of industry. But, to be fair, all lands prior to Yellowstone becoming public, used to be "publicly owned" by the indigenous peoples who inhabited them.

Vision and persistence are an effective duo toward overcoming the forces that oppose change. But sometimes a good vision and persistence need a bit more help. No doubt you've heard the quote by Thomas A. Edison, "Genius is one percent inspiration and ninety-nine percent perspiration." It turns out there is some truth in that persistence, but access to new technology can certainly be advantageous as well.

Not only was Edison persistent (he reportedly failed 5000 times before eventually succeeding at the light bulb), but he also had access to technology that solved a very specific problem that all of the light bulb inventors of the time (and there were many) grappled with.

This was that the carbon filament in a glass chamber burned up too quickly to ever become a practical light source. The key to solving this problem came from German inventor, Hermann Sprengel who invented the Sprengel pump, a vacuum pump that could evacuate the glass bulb to a near perfect vacuum.[4] That was the Edison advantage. Other inventors of the era were equally persistent and shared the vision for sustained electrified light. But, without the Edison advantage they simply couldn't implement a viable solution.

New technologies are often pathways to seeing new solutions to old problems. It used to be that in high jump competitions the dominant technique used to clear the bar was a scissor kick where the leaper would run at the bar and hoist their legs up over the bar one at a time, in essence straddling the bar.

It was important to maintain your upright position because landing on your feet was much more comfortable than landing with your head in the sand, sawdust, wood chips, or the shallow pad, that was a couple meters below.

Then, in 1965 Dick Fosbury changed the game. Instead of a scissor kick he ran toward the high jump bar and hurled himself head first, backwards, over the bar. He'd have probably broken his neck without the technological invention that helped him.

It wasn't his shoes and it wasn't a softer high jump bar (although if you've high jumped you might appreciate a softer bar). Dick Fosbury's new technique was made possible by the advent of deep foam padding. Previously, jumpers were as concerned with safely landing as they were with attaining high jump status.

Tired of losing, using the old scissor style method, Dick honed his new technique without ever obsessing over an imperfect landing. In the 1968 World Olympics in Mexico, Dick Fosbury showed his Fosbury flop technique and forever changed the sport.[5] See the endnotes for a recent Olympic interview and archived video footage of Dick Fosbury high jumping at the 1968 Olympics in Mexico City.

Sometimes an idea can catch a wave that doesn't have much to do with technology but rather a shift in sentiment or public mood. Take drugs (figuratively, not literally). Well, maybe; that depends. Please read on. After years of fighting and losing a costly "war on drugs" the public seems to be increasingly skeptical on whether that war is an effective use of public funds. It might not be cost alone that is causing the shift in public opinion. There has been much evidence around the medical benefits of marijuana, in spite of the drug being classified by the federal government as a Schedule I drug "with no currently accepted medical use and a high potential for abuse," a classification shared with LSD.[6]

And, in spite of sky high incarceration rates in the U.S. for even minor drug related offenses, most people haven't seen medical marijuana use cause Aunt Trudy to have a meltdown, become an addicted derelict, and join the ranks at the penitentiary. Much of the propaganda surrounding marijuana has been found to be inaccurate and irrelevant when citizens reflect on their own life experiences.

So, it is no wonder that citizens are pushing voter backed initiatives to decriminalize marijuana, for medical use as well as for recreational use. So far, Washington, Oregon, Colorado, Alaska, and the city of the District of Columbia have legalized recreational use of marijuana.[7]

Many others will follow, save for the states that don't offer their citizens law by the initiative process.[8] Though, in those states, the governor or legislature might want to join the "green" movement since marijuana legalization is turning Colorado into a more prosperous place with millions in new tax revenue and thousands of jobs created.[9] Go greenpreneurs!

What was literally an impossible business a few short years ago is now part of a growing industry. Thanks to the diminishing cultural and political barriers these impossipreneurs are now pot-preneurs, executing marijuana related business plans and increasing the prosperity of their communities while doing so.

I suspect the federal government will eventually catch up to the growing will of the people and decriminalize marijuana just as it did with alcohol during the repeal of prohibition.

Yes, the mood is shifting in our increasingly connected society. Truth has a way of surfacing in spite of those who wish to imprison it and keep people unknowing. Whether that truth is about the supposed dangers a drug poses to society or how financial "engineers" on Wall Street, together with their political puppets in Washington D.C., grooved together in a reckless dance that ruined a middle class and a global economy fueled by it.

People tire of the same headlines and spin especially when the stories ring untrue. Saying it's so, doesn't make it so. In a wakeful state all reasonably intelligent people will agree that you shouldn't drink murky water in spite of officials' claim that it's okay to do so.[10]

Another recent case in point. Why do agribusiness and biotech companies want to keep consumers in the dark about the genetically modified ingredients (GMOs) in food? Why do they continue to suppress efforts to force mandatory GMO labeling? It certainly isn't about making the world a better place or earth's inhabitants more healthy; it's about the money. And we are not talking about money that consumers would pay (as claimed by the GMO lobby) for clearly labeling foods containing GMOs. No, we are talking about corporate profits.

One biotech company alone, the maker of weed-killer Roundup and Roundup Ready crops, has $16 billion of revenues tied to the glyphosate-based herbicide. The main ingredient has recently been declared a probable cancer-causing product by the United Nation's cancer research center at the World Health Organization.[11] With that kind of money at stake, it's no wonder they are working hard to defeat mandatory labeling initiatives.

Most consumers are not confused on this matter and do want to know what's in the food they and their families ingest. 90 percent of mothers and 88 percent of fathers favor requiring labels for foods that have been genetically modified or contain genetically modified ingredients.[12]

It is bad enough that mega corporations want to put profits ahead of people. But, it is especially reprehensible when politicians join the mayhem. U.S. Representatives recently voted to ban GMO labeling.[13] They want to deny Americans the right to know what is in their food. While these reps will likely find themselves receiving large campaign contributions from pro GMO companies, they will also hopefully find themselves voted out of office by those citizens they claim to represent.

The truth continues to surface. Scientists have now also concluded that glyphosate is "genotoxic," meaning that it damages DNA and there's actually no safe level of exposure.[14]

Public mood is shifting. We all want much more truth and transparency and much less corruption and self dealing among society's institutions, including government, corporations and other organizations.

Perhaps we are no longer willing to look the other way given the wealth inequality in the world. Maybe it's the effects of climate change that are unmistakable and ever present. Or, the economic meltdown brought about by financial "engineers" solely interested in amassing their own good fortunes. It could also be the boomerang kids we see returning to their parents' home with student loan debt that outpaces their earning capacity and job prospects. All of these things contribute to a shifting public mood.

If we didn't experience these things firsthand, or see them happening to others with our own eyes, we are reminded of what's wrong in the world and who's to blame by cable television comedians, and even more recently by Pope Francis. In his Encyclical letter, Laudato Si', the pontiff invites every living person on the planet into a dialogue about our common home.[15] In it he says, "Politics and business have been slow to react in a way commensurate with the urgency of the challenges facing our world." He goes on to share, "Although the post-industrial period may well be remembered as one of the most irresponsible in history, nonetheless there is reason to hope that humanity at the dawn of the twenty-first century will be remembered for having generously shouldered its grave responsibilities."

The pope is not the only one growing weary of structural causes for poverty and injustice. Trickle down economic theories combined with corporations dodging taxes has created municipalities that struggle to pay the bills just like a middle class that has been systematically decimated, millions of whom remain jobless or severely underemployed.

People and communities lose when the sole focus of the corporation is on maximizing shareholder value in the short run. I think we are entering a new era where people have a heightened consciousness and are asking the questions, "What about the people? What about the environment? What about our community?" Some already do and I applaud them.

It is this distaste with the greed of the old economy that has many clamoring for what's next. We now have an old economy that is juxtaposed with a new economy. As I discovered in interviewing people while writing *The Experience Design Blueprint*, many people, especially younger workers, have had a flight to values. They've simply seen the impersonal shareholder-centric nature of corporations and know there is no loyalty, in either direction. So, many enlightened people escape corporate life altogether for one that seems more true to themselves and beneficial to others.

There is too little discussion and proposed solutions in the crossover from the old economy that is still shedding jobs and the new economy that doesn't create them fast enough or in large enough numbers.

We have been programmed to think bigger is better and unbridled growth can continue to happen. But, maybe small is the new big. I don't want bees nor do I want banks to get any larger.

I was very pleased when the City of Seattle and partners recently announced the winner for the Hack the Commute challenge. This is a hackathon put on by the City of Seattle and Commute Seattle that encouraged entrepreneurs to build solutions to fix the city's transportation issues.

The judges resisted from rewarding the team whose application showed the largest financial promise, one that might get picked up as a venture investor, and maybe one day IPO to stardom, making it founders and investors tremendously wealthy. No, instead of choosing that app and team, refreshingly, they chose a much needed app in a city rife with construction that routinely re-routes traffic and closes sidewalks. The winning team was Hackessible and their focus was on building an application that helps people in wheelchairs plan travel routes.[16]

Perhaps there is a shift in our collective thinking. Any business plan competition that I've either judged or participated in wasn't concerned with the largest social purpose or value. Instead, they dutifully and mindlessly (yes I did, too) chose the plan that could grow leaps and bounds, up and to the right, to the moon. Well, this was a refreshing departure from that old normal. The mood of people may in fact be changing.

Today's impossipreneurs are concerned with a multitude of things: values, environment, adoption of their idea, sustainability, etc. But, no matter their line of business, they face the same barriers as all of those impossipreneurs who came before them, namely, technological barriers, making a viable business, and overcoming the culture and political opposition that favors the status quo.

But, I'm optimistic. Once was a day when we had no commercial airline services, no airports. Go back further and we didn't even have aviation, or flight. Also, early in the century, wealthy owners of coal mines thought it perfectly acceptable for young boys to toil 14 hours a day on their behalf rather than attending school.

The Wright brothers solved the first problem in 1903 with the first controlled, powered and sustained human flight and President Franklin Delano Roosevelt and his administration of the progressive era solved the latter problem with the establishment of the Fair Labor Standards Act.[17][18]

We have made progress. Today, we take for granted labor laws that keep children in school instead of working. Before the minimum age of employment and hours of work for children were regulated by federal law, wealthy mine owners didn't think anything wrong with young children forgoing school in order to break large chunks of coal into smaller chunks of coal. These children were referred to as breaker boys.

Also, today we don't think much of the slow and largely invisible technological progress that has us landing safely at an airport far from our point of departure, no matter the weather, the amount of air traffic, or our in-flight encounter with an occasional flock of geese that takes out an engine.

Whether early pioneers of aviation or purveyors of reform in the progressive era these folks swam against a tide that would rather they just go with the flow of the times.

Sure, we have loads of problems today. You can find them everywhere. But, I'm optimistic. That's why I'm writing this book.

In spite of our problems, we also have many wonderful resources: a free polio vaccine, the XPRIZE whose mission is to bring about radical breakthrough for the benefit of humanity, crowdfunding platforms that get ideas visible and funded by interested parties, participatory budgeting where residents participate in a democratic process that determines how to spend part of a public budget, self publishing platforms that empower authors such as me and my father and perhaps you, blogging platforms such as

WordPress that millions have built their websites or blogs upon, Wikipedia where we can access the research and digital curation of high quality content by dedicated volunteers, the World Wide Web information space with its documents, images, and links which we all simply refer to as the Web, and communication devices (tiny computers) that fit in our pockets and that in some countries have been deployed ahead of any semblance of an electric grid.

And, while some people want things to stay the same (especially if they are doing well under the current system) many others have a curious mindset and restless human spirit that strives to make things better for themselves, and thankfully for others, too.

Impossipreneurs are all around us. Perhaps you are one. I am one. Some may look at us as impossible dreamers. I think of us as evangelists of the possible.

"It will soon be possible to transmit wireless messages around the world so simply that any individual can carry and operate his own apparatus."

Nikola Tesla
Inventor, Physicist,
Mechanical Engineer,
Electrical Engineer,
and Futurist
(1856–1943)

The future is full of opportunities. We all have the potential to do better as individuals, organizations, and communities, even the world community.

I'm proud to share the ideas in this book, whether they were conceived of by me or others during casual conversations or more formal research. What you'll find among the ideas is a common theme of *people first*. There won't be any ideas in this book about dominating others, exploiting the environment, or in general "taking advantage." This is a book for makers, not takers.

The ideas herein will face resistance. They will face technological hurdles. They will also face cultural and political barriers. Some ideas will make you laugh, other might make you angry or worrisome. I hope you find entertainment in some of the ideas. Above all, I hope they spark your imagination.

Let's start exploring some of those possibilities beginning with something near and dear to you, health and beauty.

3 HEALTH & BEAUTY

Like birds chirping away to attract a mate, humans are no less unpredictable. Men and women spend billions on health and beauty products annually. But, women by far dominate this spending category. Hispanics in the U.S. spend more than any other ethnicity.[1] Brazilians, though only 3 percent of the world's population make up 12 percent of deodorant consumption, the highest in the world. Its citizens also spend more money on perfume than any other nation.[2]

This isn't just about personal hygiene and grooming this is hardwired DNA behavior that has us competing for mates.

Even during economic downturns, women in particular, are more likely to buy beauty products. Researchers refer to this as the "lipstick effect": The more insecure the economy, the more money women spend on beauty products.[3] This can be to attract partners who are financially secure. Individually and probably subconsciously, it feels like a good investment. Collectively, this ensures the survival of our species.

The irony is that even past the point of being able to

procreate, the spending on health and beauty products doesn't plateau, it actually increases. In the U.K., women over 50 are now the largest spender on beauty products.[4] In later years, the shift is more likely toward creature comforts such as lotions and potions and anti-aging products. Older women are also more likely to treat themselves to spa visits, treatments, and cosmetic surgery of all types. It's no surprise, older women strive to look and feel younger. And, cosmetic companies are there to promote this, by spending enormous amounts of money on advertising. The L'Oreal Paris slogan captures the sentiment of many women when it comes to beauty spending, "Because I'm Worth It!"[5]

Let's examine some impossible ideas that if brought to life could make us feel even more healthy and more beautiful. Let's look beyond effective ad slogans.

Personal Chemist. The Personal Chemist is a complete make-up system personalized to your skin type, chemistry, and desired skin tone. Using digital imaging technology you can visualize yourself in different "moods" on screen and then select the look that marks your desired mood. The Personal Chemist then suggests the formulaic components needed, taking into account your allergies and skin conditions. The system also makes use of your location so if the forecast is for hot and sunny, then you'll find sunscreen as part of the mix.

Users of the Personal Chemist not only look their best, but they also are doing the best they can for their skin. The system tracks usage and changing skin conditions and adjusts its formula accordingly. The system uses raw, food grade, and organic ingredients known for their anti-aging effects and rejuvenating properties.

With Personal Chemist you can see images of what you would look like ahead of any purchase commitment, long before you visit the studio (traditionally, the store).

Make-up Chem-artist. Once in the studio you're greeted by a Make-up Chem-artist who reviews your digital profile and further assists you. Your formulaic components are mixed and bottled for immediate application or later application in the convenience of your home.

Make-up and Potion Printer. Once you've successfully learned how the Personal Chemist make-up system works in studio, you become authorized to print refill-bottles at home using a Make-up and Potion Printer. Though your Make-up Chem-artist is always there to assist you, be confident you can recreate the necessary make-up components in the convenience of your home.

Dream Cream allows people, especially women, to sculpt their body by applying a specially formulated cream to the areas they wish to redistribute. This is a two part cream, *melt away* to reduce certain areas and *enhance*, the areas that you wish to bulk up. With Dream Cream women literally take weight off of their hips and butts and redistribute it to their breasts. Breasts are a likely desired destination for this redistribution. Among American women in 2013 there were 290,000 breast augmentation surgeries performed.[6]

Men could eliminate those beer guts and jelly rolls around their middles and bulk up their skinny legs or undeveloped chests. Now those men and women that appear wiry could bulk up a bit to prevent blowing over in the wind.

Hair Gel Restoration. Most people think of men when they think of balding. After all, you haven't likely heard the female equivalent term of male-pattern baldness. But, women are affected by thinning hair as well. If you are a woman with thinning hair, you know firsthand that it thins all over, unlike in most males. While men might "suck it up," do the comb over, or cover up with a baseball cap, for women it can be more emotionally devastating.

Hair Gel Restoration changes this. Rub the hair gel onto the affected areas of the scalp. The gel does two things. First it adds genetic material, or transgenes, to the affected area. This material is harvested naturally through a donor program similar to people that graciously donate plasma. Secondly, the gel awakens the existing hair follicles. Then when phototherapy (light of certain wavelength, intensity, and dose) is applied to the gelled area it stimulates continued cell metabolism. The gel and light work together in a nonsurgical solution to produce cosmetically significant hair restoring women's beauty and men's youthful confidence.

Hair and skin have always been an important part of our appearance, but so have teeth and fashion. On the surface all of this seems like harmless adornments but it wasn't always see this way. In 1770, an act was introduced in English Parliament that would make it illegal for women to use scents, paints, artificial teeth, false hair and even high-heeled shoes to lure men into marriage. Those found guilty under this law would be tried for witchcraft and the marriages annulled.

Well, in spite of many books and articles citing the act there is no evidence it was ever fully signed into law.[7] Beauty and fashion remained a focus for many, however controversial and polarizing.

As much as people have been and continue to be concerned about outward beauty, inner physical and mental health reigns supreme. If you don't believe that, then you've probably not known a physically beautiful person who suffers from mental illness or a terminal disease that leaves their appearance harmonious, but turns their inside state hostile and even incompatible. Sadly, I've known several and have friends in this category as I write this.

Before we get to the inner beauty let's focus on ideas for the functional pearls that adorn our smiles.

Oral Prophet. This complete oral health care system deviates from the mere evolution of the toothbrush. Manual brushing still suffers from poor technique, consistency of habit, and lack of sensing ability. Today's toothbrushes in all their vibrating glory are still dumb objects devoid of our oral history and or current state of health.

The Oral Prophet goes beyond a brush to report our current state of health and foretell developing problems. Once fitted to your mouth and put to use, its brushing train of bristles vibrates to clean and polish your teeth. It doesn't quit prematurely because it has something else on its mind or because it's arm became tired. It's chief concern is your oral health.

The Oral Prophet senses the microbes in your mouth, actually your entire oral cavity of tongue, gums, roof of mouth, and teeth. It records what it finds as it performs its flawless operation. The system builds your oral history and provides early detection of problems in your mouth or elsewhere in your body. Did you know that your mouth provides a window into your overall health? Nearly 9 of 10 diseases can cause symptoms in your mouth.[8] To date, oral bacteria have been implicated in cardiovascular disease, pancreatic cancer, colorectal cancer, rheumatoid arthritis, and preterm birth, among other things.[9]

The data collected from the Oral Prophet is available to you, your healthcare professionals, and in abstract form to the larger research effort that aims to fill the void of research linking epigenetics and oral health, projects such as the Human Oral Microbiome Database.[10]

Epigenetics Primer
Almost every cell in our bodies has the same DNA

sequence, but not all cells are the same. That is because different cells use the code in different ways.

Stuff happens to the genes during development and through life. They are turned on and off depending on their jobs.[11]

The human genome is the complete assembly of DNA (deoxyribonucleic acid) — about 3 billion base pairs — that makes each individual unique. DNA holds the instructions for building the proteins that carry out a variety of functions in a cell.

The epigenome is made up of chemical compounds and proteins that can attach to DNA and direct such actions as turning genes on or off, controlling the production of proteins in particular cells.[12]

The changes in organisms are caused by modification of gene expression rather than alteration of the genetic code (DNA) itself. Epigenetic changes are what makes a brain cell different than a heart cell or hair cell, even though the underlying genetic code is the same. Epigenetic changes are chemical tweaks to the DNA and to the proteins that package our DNA. They don't necessarily affect genes themselves, they affect particular regions of the code whose job it is to turn genes on or off.[13] Think of the epigenome as the record of the changes to the genes.

Epigenetics is the study of changes in organisms caused by modification of gene expression rather than alteration of the genetic code itself. Epigenetics plays a role in cancer, development, disease, etc. A cell responds to external stimuli by changing its epigenetics.[14] Epigenetics includes the study of these external or environmental factors that turn genes "on" and "off" and affect how cells "read" genes.

This means we don't just inherit our biology we also impact our biology through our state of mind, what we ingest, and our level of exercise – mind, mouth, and muscle.[15] This is a big deal. Some diseases are linked with epigenetic changes. In cancer for example, a condition where cells replicate out of control, scientist see rogue epigenetic changes. These change are linked to genes behaving weirdly. Genes being expressed that shouldn't be expressed. Or, genes shut off that usually keep cells in check.[16]

DNA is not destiny, your life choices are. As explained by Associate Professor Hughes from the University of Adelaide's School of Dentistry, "Our genetic code, or DNA, is like an orchestra – it contains all of the elements we need to function – but the epigenetic code is essentially the conductor, telling which instruments to play or stay silent, or how to respond at any given moment."[17]

If certain genes get over expressed you might become ill. That is when traditional medicine steps in to treat the symptoms. We can choose to be on autopilot, ignoring how our decisions impact our health and longevity, but we might not like the resultant sounds that our symphony's produce.

Likewise, by paying attention to these factors, our human bodies may in fact be upgradeable.

No matter your genes, your epigenomes, and your mind, mouth, and muscle habits, not everybody will be have thick red hair, full lips, and be able to run a 3 minute mile. Besides, even if you start your life journey with all of that, you won't have it forever. Aging happens. And, unless you're a giant sequoia that doesn't have a natural terminus to its life, your cells will eventually age and die.

The Giant Sequoia
As I shared in *The Experience Design Blueprint*, the giant sequoia is the only natural living organism that doesn't have a natural terminus to its life; old age just keeps getting older

for the giant sequoia.[18][19] All other plants and animals undergo changes at the cellular level, as they mature and eventually die. A giant sequoia properly supported and shielded from insects, fires, and other damage will literally live forever. It turns out; they usually fall under their own weight, which then prompts further decay.[20]

Bob, a friend of mine in his nineties said to me, "The other day I tried to run to see if I still could." He then added, "That wasn't a good idea." Bob has the wisdom to accept his limitations. But, what exactly are our limitations. For that, we could use a few ideas that look at our inner health.

Beauty is more than skin deep anyway, right? Our insides are important as well. Our inner beauty is our health. So let's start there. Let's explore ideas that concern our inner beauty.

Life Expectancy Ticker. This life changing monitor continuously records your activities and consumption. It gives you a real time assessment of life expectancy. It also shares with you the underlying details. With it, you might think twice about eating or drinking some of the food and beverages that you now consume without concern. If you have a nasty tobacco habit, the Life Expectancy Ticker might just convince you to finally quit. Maybe you'll choose moderation or ignore altogether its "That's enough cookies (or cigarettes, or alcohol) for you!" message. I know, you're already hoping there is a "cookie snooze" button.

Daily Diagnosis System. Imagine each morning upon waking you put on a few sensors, don a little cap, and breath into a tube. The Daily Diagnosis System tells you how you are doing physiologically. Alongside the system's comprehensive analysis, it also suggests specific things to address for the day, e.g., walk 4,000 more steps than yesterday, eat a banana to boost your potassium, etc. In the event something more severe is going on a healthcare professional or family member is contacted. Data is collected and an accurate history is recorded. You can optionally add in information about your habits, or connect those from ancillary devices such as smartphones or other wellness appliances.

See also: Sampling Commode

Monitor Me. This is a tiny wearable device that monitors your health in real time, analyzes the findings, and stores the results in your comprehensive personal medical history. This solves the information deficit that you have about your own body. You can search the Web for information of all types but you can't retrieve anything about your own body. You don't know anything until you visit a healthcare facility. What's the first thing they do? Check your vital signs. Now you can fast forward through that step with Monitor Me, the solution that puts all those monitoring machines and devices of the emergency room into a tiny body worn device.

It is the early warning system for our own bodies that brings down the cost of care for everybody. It is like having a tiny built in physician. Monitor Me continuously exams your heart rate and rhythm, blood pressure, temperature, respiratory rate, blood oxygen level. It even checks for stress. Using Monitor Me can help you reduce stress, optimize your daily performance, lose weight, improve sleep and find more calm in your life.

Monitor Me not only analyzes and stores vital information, it also connects. In the event of a seizure, stroke, heart attack, or other emergency or accident, Monitor Me connects you to an emergency network and using location services, will alert life saving personnel that can be dispatched to provide assistance. When emergency medical technicians arrive they'll already be informed of your medical history and vitals and be ready to treat you.

Medical Advisor is an artificial intelligence medical information system that works in concert with Oral Prophet, Daily Diagnosis, and Monitor Me. The system detects subtle physiological changes and alerts you to developing patterns before you detect them. It can tell you allergies before you consciously recognize any symptoms. It is based on your unique genetic profile and your historic and real time health data.

Medical professionals also use Medical Advisor to determine courses of treatment that are personalized to your unique profile, but that are informed by the massive data available in other patients treated with similar symptoms and profiles. The system also contains intelligent access to clinical trials, natural remedies, medications, and courses of therapy. Medical Advisor is more informed than any doctor could be and it is less prone to human error. Medical Advisor is a doctor's best assistant. With Medical Advisor, healthcare becomes more personalized, more relevant, more effective and less costly for all of us.

Magnetic Cancer Stick. Imagine cancer cells could be tricked to become attracted to a certain location, away from the brain's motor strip or other vital organs and cells. Imagine these tricked cancerous cells migrated toward this location, much like iron filings are attracted to a strong magnet. Once the cells become attracted to and migrate toward the Magnetic Cancer Stick they can be isolated and annihilated in place or removed without harming other cells necessary for normal life function. Good bye cancer, hello living.

Exercise is a beauty booster so a chapter on health and beauty would be incomplete without an "impossible" idea surrounding the notion of exercise.

Happy Robot Nag is your companion robot who is

tireless and purely devoted to your exercise regime. It doesn't ever annoy like a loving spouse or coach might. It's Spock-like (R.I.P. Leonard Nimoy) in its keep cool, logical, objective, recording of your physical activity. But, Happy Robot Nag also has a playful demeanor. It will challenge you to become the best YOU. No more blind spots, no short cuts, or abandoned workouts. Happy Robot Nag is your workout taskmaster. You set the goals and it sets the plan in motion. Together you live long and prosper.

In *The Experience Design Blueprint*, I state things happen gradually even though we might not be paying attention to them. Consider the Day Old Bread Theory.

Day Old Bread Theory

Have you ever caught yourself thinking or saying aloud, "The bread should be fine, it was good yesterday?" It is true most days; the bread is good until the day that it's not. But, then one day the bread, suddenly and surprisingly goes bad.

We treat other areas of our lives much like we do aging bread. Because we don't visibly see things gradually changing, doesn't mean they don't. I have a wonderful friend and mother-in-law (R.I.P. Karen) who was diagnosed and eventually died from a cancerous brain tumor that wouldn't let up. Prior to being diagnosed, things were obviously changing beneath the surface of what we could see. Symptoms that Karen experienced and family members witnessed were explained away, much like the dust forming on the metamorphosing bread.

In other areas of our lives beside bread, we unknowingly apply this same theory. Bread and other things do change. We are either moving too quickly to recognize gradual changes or we explain things away until the day we become shocked that things are not what they once were. This applies to everything from bicycle and vehicle maintenance to our own health issues. In Chapter 8 of that same book I talk about establishing "sensors in the ground" to detect changes before it is too late. You might already be thinking about organizations that have lost their way as the world outside "suddenly" changed right under their noses. History is full of such organizations that became out of touch with their audiences.

It is best to record the data and learn from it. Let's empower public policy makers and innovative entrepreneurs (or impossipreneurs) with aggregate health data so they can make policy and innovative products and services to benefit us all.

Data collected would be without an agenda that favors any corporation or anything other than simply surfacing of the truth. If brain cancer or muscular dystrophy are disproportionately high in a particular region then let the data be passively collected over time and examined to see why that is the case.

If we find that excessive cell phone use on cloudy days or standing in front of a microwave installed over the stove is causing irreparable harm to the tissues in our heads, then lets expose those issues so people can make more informed decisions. Let's not suppress data to protect corporate interests, especially when impossipreneurs can design new methods and objects free of negative effects.

Over time, aggregated data from many individuals can inform a wide range of public health questions that can benefit all of humanity. I say, let the dataset change our mindset.

"Without data you're just another person with an opinion."

William Edwards Deming
American engineer, author
statistician, professor, lecturer,
and management consultant.
(1900–1993)

Chapter Summary

This chapter began with data in the form of beauty statistics. We then went beyond our exteriors to explore new possibilities given the advances in the human genome project and epigenetics. It is hard to imagine solutions to health care problems without first imagining data.

Data is a big deal if we pay attention to it. It can measure progress, but it can also inspire us to create policies, and programs to move that data in the right direction. Data is the reality that can disprove long held myths, whether those myths are about the solar system, the environment, or our health. As a society we'll have to increase our trust, overcome privacy paranoia, and detect and immediately remedy any violations. The benefits of data are too important are far-reaching for us to remain trapped in safe ignorance.

No matter if we are concerned with outward beauty or inward beauty and whether we are here on earth for a short while or a long while (like my nonagenarian friend Bob) the fact is most of us would rather dance with somebody than dance alone.

Our next chapter gives us a fresh look at love and relationships and some ideas that if we could make them happen would benefit us all.

4 LOVE & RELATIONSHIPS

When you think of harmonious relationships, I'm curious, what comes to mind? Is it flowers and chocolates, marriage, soul mates, dating, anniversary parties, or something else? Each of these things has romantic connotations. Perhaps you were thinking more of business relationships or other types of relationships.

But, what does an improving relationship look like, or one that isn't as good as another? You're probably coming up short about now.

Mental models are images, representations, or schemes of how we perceive and understand the world around us. Like all models, mental models are abstractions of reality. Mental models help shape behavior and set an approach to solving problems and doing tasks.[1]

If you are like most people, you have a pretty clear mental model for chopping wood, but your mental model for maintaining harmonious relationships is missing. You probably haven't spent much time imagining what this looks like. That is bad news because your life is probably more dependent upon healthy relationships than it is on chopping wood.

Relationships between people are what makes schools, governments, churches, businesses, even families function. The better the relationships between people, the more likely it is that they will work well together and feel a sense of accomplishment. One only need look at partisan politics or dysfunctional families to see progress stalled and possibilities halted.

We observe that some people seem to be good at navigating and building relationships while others are not. Whether they are lucky in love in their personal relationship or seem to just plain get along with everybody in business and on teams, some people appear to have the knack for harmonious relationships whereas others truly struggle.

Imagine we all were adept at navigating relationships of all types so that we could be more peaceful, more productive, and more prosperous. That would be a good thing, right? Well, good for all, save for the divorce lawyers and conflict counselors.

Sometimes relationships appear good at the start, but then they decay over time. We somehow lose our way. Like having a map helps you navigate unfamiliar territory, we need a mental model to help us demystify the complexity around relationships and then guide us toward improving them.

Chances are you're not only unable to describe your mental model for relationships, you also can't show how they improve, become worse, or end.

The Spiralometer is a mental model that changes this. Imagine a double helix, interwoven like a DNA strand. There are two strands in the weave, each representing a person in the relationship. How tightly the two strands are woven represents how close the people are, in terms of interaction points. If there are not very many interactions then the strands are loosely coupled. With your closest friends, you have more interaction points.

The first step toward improving or maintaining relationships is to increase the number of interaction points. Ever heard the little voice inside you saying to call mom or call that friend? Imagine having such suggestions for interaction points that could improve our relationships, especially those important ones that for the moment are at risk of falling into neglect.

While quantity of interaction is a factor in healthy relationships so is the quality of the interactions. Relationships are never static. Whether they are of a personal or business nature, they are either improving or they are getting worse. Picture this as the Spiralometer, rotating, spinning upward or downward. The rate of ascent or descent may be slow and steady or fast. We all like to feel our relationships ascending smoothly and getting healthier over time.

Imagine having suggested actions to keep a relationship ascending and getting healthier. And, in the event our relationship is in decline we would benefit knowing what to do, in order to turn it around or at least slow the descent. We need the equivalent of road signs and signals for our relationships before things turn intolerably bad.

You have a Spiralometer for every relationship in your life. Some are tightly coupled and long standing, others loosely coupled and only beginning. Some are ascending while others are descending. By using the mental model of the Spiralometer you can visualize the state of your relationships.

Visualizing your relationships enables you to think about how to improve them. It also better prepares you to have healthy conversations about them. This is useful because your relationships are most certainly more important for you than chopping wood.

Certain Step. Imagine a relationship in trouble. Your

Spiralometer is descending downward. You may have no interest in turning it around. When you've reached this point, you've reached your point of no return. You might have a relationship in your life like this right now. Or, maybe you did in the past. You likely will in the future. Sometimes, you feel that you need to escape or avoid contact with a person altogether. Maybe somebody suddenly turned dangerously bad. But, what if you are wrong?

Wouldn't it be nice to have such an early warning system for our relationships. A system that tells us with certainty that things can be worked out, or they cannot and we should step away and move on. Certain Step is such an early warning system. As we go about living our lives Certain Step gives us audible signals like the undercover spy who receives sage step-by-step instructions and advice through an invisible earpiece. Instructions can also be hidden in plain sight, embedded in the Bluetooth earpiece many already wear. Visual learners benefit from the ocular overlay in glasses or contact form, which creates a virtual image superimposed on the ordinary viewable world. These visual cues are completely hidden from others.

Now, you can have clarity of thought and confidence in the next step taken. Think of this as the "perfect match" solution when you might not have the perfect match, whether the relationship is personal or business. Use Certain Step to improve existing relationships or escape when it is time to move on.

Evade Now. Similar to Certain Step, Evade Now is a mode reserved for those special cases where some people are best detected in order to avoid them. This could easily be called Creep Detect.

There is no shortage of headlines and criminally focused television shows that remind us of the bad among the good. In such cases, our early warning system needs to alert us to potential danger. With Evade Now when we are nearing a person of nefarious character or ill intention, we get expert instructions on exactly how to extricate ourselves from the situation.

This is a bit like the anti-collision system in a vehicle that applies brakes when the radar detects an object approaching too quickly. Throughout human history, our intuition has played this role for our own self preservation. But, in a noisy, crowded world, full of biases (our own and media reinforced), our pattern making machines a.k.a. our brains, often do read situations and people incorrectly. One only need look at officer involved shootings in the United States to see this firsthand.[2]

See also: Jury Sound Dome and Karmic Sensing Bullets

Evade Now knows the difference between fact and fiction, imagination and reality. Use Evade Now to nullify the effects of sociopaths and criminals before they can inflict harm on you.

Correcto Brain. Throughout our lives we make mistakes. And, as we make more mistakes their cumulative effects stack up and reinforce our earlier mistakes. The same system that gives us Certain Step and Evade Now can be used to improve our thinking and behaviors.

Correcto Brain begins to unravel the uncomfortable fabric of self illusion and deception. It returns us to a fact based reality so we can live more harmoniously with ourselves and among others.

To reduce our thinking errors and biases we need real time feedback for when they occur. After all, practice makes perfect, not training. Correcto Brain provides that real-time feedback in audible and visual form. It's like the life assistant that nudges us toward reality when we start to drift into an imaginary world.

See also: Truth Ticker

Commitment Meter. Imagine joining forces with a partner, whether in a personal relationship or as part of a team, and then finding out that while you were 100 percent committed, they were much less so. Maybe they were 50 percent committed or 10 percent, or not at all. You'd eventually find out through their actions, or rather, inaction. But, waiting can be harmful. The Commitment Meter gives you a real time record of the commitment levels of the people involved in personal and business relationships.

When you commit your heart and soul 100 percent into a relationship the other person can feel it. The Commitment Meter shows this, the other person feels it and this can, in turn, motivate them to shift their energy and passion, too. If they don't, then at least you have an early warning system that informs your decision to bail or stay involved.

Imagine having a Commitment Meter to show the level of engagement for every person on a team. Imagine these biosensors were built into the conference table. The meter in the middle of the table shows the relative commitment of each person. Without such a meter, you're operating blindly and leaving your desired outcomes to chance.

Mother Tongue Translator. At times, relationships can suffer because of poor understanding. This might be due to language barriers. The Mother Tongue Translator operates as a real time translator much like a Web browser can translate a Web page. This gives people the ability to communicate with each other when language or accents prevent effective communication. The translator also indicates the words that are not readily translatable, so people can understand when they are not being understood. It gives people the opportunity to rephrase. After all, we speak to be understood, not simply to be heard. With the Mother Tongue Translator new relationships can be built and existing ones improved. I imagine if Helen Keller were alive today, she might be involved in such a project.

Theaetetus of Athens asked Socrates to
define thought.

Socrates replied,
"The talk which the soul has with itself."

Thoughts From a Wireless Brain. Look outside your window. Do you see any ants? No. Does that mean there aren't any ants? Of course not. As you are reading this your neurons are firing, there is electrical activity going on inside of your brain. Nobody outside of you sees this happening inside of your head. But like the ants, your neurons are busy working.

Is it possible to detect ants outside your window? Yes, but not with your naked eye; you need a little help. Likewise your eyes are not able to directly see brain signals. For that, today you need to rely on an array of electrodes that are sensitive to the subtle voltage oscillations caused by the firing groups of neurons, the basic building blocks of your brain. As sensing technology improves and we develop better algorithms to discard noisy interference, we'll unleash new understanding about the brain, and with it, a host of opportunities.

Until then our impossipreneur ideas will remain trapped, albeit temporarily. Here are a few of my favorite ideas that once mastered could seriously improve our relationships and human progress that depends upon them.

Spouse Aware (Beware). For most people it's difficult to imagine a bright future without sharing it with loved ones. But, sometimes it's our loved ones that are the source of frustration. Or, dare I say it, we frustrate those we love.

This early detection system lets you know what's really bothering your spouse, even when they are not able to, or choose not to, clearly articulate what is bothering them. What's wrong honey? "Oh nothing" Uh huh – slowly retreating yeah – heard that one before. With the step-by-step instructions received from Spouse Aware you know exactly how to remedy the situation and keep or restore the peace in your relationship.

Spouse Aware makes use of thought sensing technology in conjunction with the audible and ocular features of the Certain Step and Evade Now system.

Cochlea Isolation Mute. If you can hear a sound you should be able to tune it out. That is the idea behind noise canceling headphones. But, what if the noise you want to tune out is your neighbor's barking dog, the jet passing overhead, or an enraged spouse or colleague?

We've all been there. Listening to someone in a meeting that takes the group to a place called nowhere. They are disruptive, off topic, and paying attention to their own agenda with little concern for others' time. Well, no need to tolerate this any longer. With Cochlea Isolation Mute you can silence them simply by looking directly at them to establish the direction of the offending sound, then say "rant mute" to begin isolating the sound to be muted.

They become inaudible except to themselves. While your group goes about its business at hand, the perpetrator, once muted, hears only their own voice, as though they are in a deep sea dive helmet. The ineffectual reverberation of their own voice will continuously annoy them until eventually they realize that they've been muted. Rant Mute also works on disruptive spouses, children, parents, and bosses.

Truth Detective Mouth Arrestor. Relationships can especially suffer when we are not truthful. Think of the Truth Detective Mouth Arrestor as a mouth zipper that has many warnings before it corrects the mind by forcing the muscles around the mouth to "zip it" closed. Upon detecting a spoken statement as untrue, the arrestor issues an internally audible alert. Think of this as the little voice inside your head that says, "That's not true." As the subject keeps talking they receive more audible alerts, "Not true. Not true Stop saying it. Not true. Yup, still not true. Nope, that's not true. Nope. 1st warning. Not true. 2nd warning. Not true. Zzzzzip."

Marriage Wears. Following their nuptials, newly married couples begin wearing Marriage Wears, the undergarments that record physiological changes, and specifically temptations, throughout the day for later playback when married couples can engage in "healthy" dinner table conversation. "Dear, let talk about what you were thinking at 10:30 this morning."

Companion Match. Like the employment talent match, everybody should have somebody. So, there is a matching service for that. In the future, nobody is lonely.

Portable Hole. In the event there appears to be no remedying a bad situation with your spouse use the portable hole to escape. This concept is inspired by the 1955 Looney Tunes cartoon directed by Robert McKimson. In it, the main character, Professor Calvin Q. Calculus successfully invents a portable hole. It is shown to have a wide range of uses, not the least of which is escaping from a nagging spouse. You can either escape into the hole yourself or place it in the path of your unsuspecting spouse. Either way, you get some sorely needed respite. Check out the original cartoon by searching online for "The Hole Idea."

Cognitive Overload Detect. We've all been there, trying to learn too much, too quickly. Or, maybe we were the person teaching. Whether the situation is about a new job, a class, or researching a new subject, it is useful when we fully absorb the information that we're attempting to learn. When the information comes too quickly, we don't absorb it and it feels as though we are drinking from the fire hose.

Imagine each of us has a digital recorder for our mind – a Tivo of sorts. We could slow down the action, pause it, fast forward the parts we don't care about or already know, all in an effort to improve our comprehension. Also, imagine that we detected when we were starting to get behind or were going too fast and not fully absorbing the information. This is also important for teachers to know. How much more effective would the classroom or training facility be if the teacher really knew how each student was progressing?

See also: Bank-a-Thought and Memory Search

Chapter Summary
This chapter gave us a fresh look at love and relationships. We explored some ideas that if fully blossomed would make relationships of all types more harmonious.

Hopefully this chapter made you think about new possibilities for relationships. I hope you envision the Spiralometer so clearly that you can explain it to another person. I hope you actually do.

As author, political activist, and lecturer, Helen Keller said, "Alone we can do so little. Together we can do so much." Since Helen was deafblind from the age of 19 months old, I am certain that she valued harmonious human relationships. After all, with the help of her instructor and lifelong companion, Anne Sullivan, Helen was able to attend and graduate cum laude from Radcliffe College in 1904.

Helen didn't know the meaning of impossible. She was the first person who was deafblind to write a book. Her autobiography, *The Story of My Life*, was the first of 14 books she wrote in her lifetime.

In the 1940s and 1950s, Helen Keller visited 39 countries to persuade their governments to establish schools for people who were blind and deaf. Many countries did just that, and Keller is revered around the world to this day.[3]

"The most important day I remember in all
my life is the one on which my teacher,
Anne Mansfield Sullivan,
came to me.

I am filled with wonder when I consider
the immeasurable contrast between
the two lives which it connects."

Helen Adams Keller
American author, political activist, and lecturer
(1880–1968)

5 WEALTH & ECONOMY

We live in an abundant world, but at the same time we face scarcity as individuals, communities, and even entire countries. No matter what your socio-economic status you would have to be completely inobservant to not notice the divide between those doing well and those left behind in an economy that relentlessly grinds forward. And, no matter your socio-economic status at this moment, it can change quickly. If and when it does change, it will probably not be for reasons within your control. Chalk up those future changes to the same culprits that have negatively affected people before, changes to their health, their employment status, and depending on which country you're in, the safety net that is disappearing or already decimated. Add to this the reckless work of self-interested financial "engineers" and politicians, and there is cause for concern.

Though there is no wealth and economy without people, it begs the question "What about the people?" Why is there nary a mention in corporate behavior, political discourse, or media that covers both.

At the time of this writing within the European Union, Greece is feeling pressure from richer countries such as Germany to meet its debt obligations. Perhaps one of the shortcomings of the EU is that there is no real mechanism for money to flow from richer countries to poorer countries.

The United States, while rife with its own problems, doesn't have this particular problem. Here is why. While some states are clearly richer than other states, in the U.S. it is different because money does flow from richer states to poorer states, though not directly. The U.S. federal government requires a federal income tax from people in all 50 states. So, money flows toward the federal government and then it is redistributed outward to poor states to help fund education, healthcare, social security, transportation, etc.[1]

Without such a mechanism some of the poorer states in the union may have failed by now. But, just because there hasn't been insolvent states doesn't mean that municipalities haven't gone bankrupt; many have.[2] Individuals and companies have too, of course.

In the broader world stage there are developed nations and developing nations. The concern of the former is economic growth, while the concern for the latter is economic development. What would be good for all of the planets inhabitants would be for redistribution to happen between developing and developed nations. But, when we think of redistribution at a planetary level, it's hard to imagine it working, right?

Of course it is because is lies outside our sphere of concern. When we think of our own personal economies most of us don't think so much of developing nations. The exception is when we answer the call of the occasional disaster relief campaign or need a good cause in order to shave a few dollars from our tax liabilities. Still then, many people prefer to support local causes over those afar.

Although many would like to not concern themselves with the developing world or even economies in neighboring countries, we all do share a planet. And, since none of our countries contain all of the means of production for all of the things we desire, at some level we need to trade and collaborate.

After all, that is how you are able to eat your chocolate bar, access the Internet on your smartphone, and write on your computer. As I am writing this I'm drinking coconut water extracted from young coconuts in Thailand that I purchased at Costco. But, I'm also drinking coffee that was sourced another continent away. Supply chains already connect us but not in highly visible ways that the Internet and social media do. The boundaries that keep us isolated from each other include differences in currency, language, and governments though the Internet attempts (and often succeeds) at squashing these barriers.

Isolationism of the past has proven to be dangerous as visionary dictators ran roughshod over people and nations. Add to the dictators, greedy companies seeking profits at all costs, and to the environment, people and nations, and there is cause for concern.

We can do better. We usually do when there is a major crisis. But, the key is to not be ruled by disasters and crises. Let's intentionally design the world we want to live in and leave behind.

Poverty anywhere constitutes a danger to prosperity everywhere.

A more prosperous people is sorely needed in the world, if for no other reason than stability. Like the proverb says, an idle brain is the devil's workshop.

We need a more equitable economy. We really want and need as Buckminster Fuller said, a world that works for everyone with no one and nothing left out.

"Make the world work, for 100% of humanity, in the shortest possible time, through spontaneous cooperation, without ecological offense or the disadvantage of anyone."

Richard Buckminster "Bucky" Fuller
American architect, systems theorist,
author, designer, and inventor
(1895–1983)

Something to think about while you read this chapter is what is an economic system, really? Who should it serve and what should people's roles be in the economy over the course of their lives? What about the role of institutions, governments, companies, and organizations of all types and sizes? This chapter provides potential solutions to make a more equitable world.

This chapter attempts to offer a fresh look at tired problems. It is an attempt to provoke thought, change the conversation, and exert new economic pressure points.

The pressure points are necessary to create a more prosperous and harmonious world society as opposed to supporting current methods and thinking that brings about more strife and stunted opportunities for many, while a few do extremely well.

One View of the Truth. When tackling problems or addressing opportunities of any sort, it helps to start with one view of the truth. Nothing works for all of us if we are not operating from One View of the Truth.

One of the challenges we face together is that we have to overcome the biases and false beliefs as discussed in the last chapter. If giant sequoias could talk they may in fact laugh at us, shaking their towering heads and pointing their branchy fingers, "Ha ha ha, you humans never seem to learn. There is much talking but little learning."

Truth Sculpture. Imagine that as we explored a subject we could visualize it in three dimensions. We would nudge toward the truth, chipping away at a problem or opportunity until the Truth Sculpture emerges. Facts would be shown and unfounded opinions and arguments stripped away or never to appear in the first place. Anyone could participate in building a Truth Sculpture, either by adding facts or by nominating a problem, issue, or statement to be explored.

Once initiated, data is put forth and more truths exposed (facts not opinions) until finally something that resembles reality emerges. No marketing spin, no political hyperbole, or relativity of truth so elegantly framed from sophists; just plain speak and simple facts. Is Sodium Nitrite necessary in your food today? I suspect not, but let's build a Truth Sculpture and see what emerges. What would you like to have explored? How different do you think the outcomes of courtrooms would be or public policies?

Once we have the fact based reality in the form of a Truth Sculpture we can then distribute it for others to see. We have data, we have distributed systems, let us set the truth free for all of us to see.

But, even when we see the truth plainly in front of us, some people still never accept or recognize it as truth. For these people we need to address what I believe to be our public enemy number one. No, it's not terrorism. It's also not ignorance either, though that is a runner up. Here is a clue. It is a skill that many are lacking. Give up? Turn the page for the answer.

The number one skill that people are lacking is empathy. It is our ability to understand and feel what it must be like to walk in another person's moccasins or high heels or bare feet, or to understand what it's like to have no feet at all. When we are unempathetic we can't possibly understand the perspective of another person. We don't recognize their feelings, their context, or point of view. Each of us has experienced a lack of empathy when a bureaucracy incompetently and unapologetically cited policy and then summarily dismissed us, denied us, disrespected us, or whatever else they did to us. They may also have simply ignored us.

Empathy Builder. We are communal by nature yet when we don ear buds and bury ourselves in front of screens of all sizes we avoid real discussion and face-to-face interaction. Most of the media we are exposed to serves to enflame not inform us. The bad is dramatically sensationalized while progress and great things go unreported. We no longer visit video stores or interact with bank tellers. We buy online and pay at the pump. We are having less and less human interactions. And, we especially don't have those interactions with people not like us.

So, when news surfaced of a 6-year-old boy name Jaden Hayes being on a mission to make people smile that looked sad, I felt the need to share it.

Jaden was sad himself having lost his father and more recently his mother who died in her sleep. The little boy shared with his aunt and guardian, "I'm sick and tired of seeing everybody sad all of the time." He told her that he had a plan to change that. With her assistance he's been targeting people in downtown Savannah, Georgia. He locates people that aren't smiling and then gives them a small toy such as a rubber ducky or a dinosaur, expecting nothing in return, except perhaps a smile. It's working. He has counted nearly 500 unsuspecting "smilers" and he shared with Steve Hartman of CBS news that he's going for 33,000.[3]

This kid is lifting spirits in Savannah, Georgia. Imagine if all of us did even a fraction as much as this young boy.

The Empathy Builder is the path to do just that. It restores our communal nature and builds connection to others not like us. Imagine connecting and conversing with people in other countries or even parts of your own country, or unfamiliar parts of your own city.

With Empathy Builder you make local or planetary friends and then better understand what it is like to be them. You get to experience life as they do, know firsthand their context, their ups and downs, opportunities and struggles, frustration, and moments of elation. You increase your own cultural sensitivity along the way. Choose among planetary friends in politically unstable or economically challenged nations or from regions that boast more prosperity than yours.

Using Empathy Builder you can broaden your perspective, increase your knowledge of other cultures, and sharpen your world view. Built-in gamification principles encourage learning opportunities and recognize and reward your achievements and newly demonstrated competencies.

You might recall a time when you were young and exchanged letters with a pen pal. With Empathy Builder you gain the benefits of a traditional pen pal, but you are also able to take advantage of technology that has created an expanded world for us all.

Using the Mother Tongue Translator discussed in the previous chapter you are able to fluidly understand your new planetary friends even when you don't share a common language.

The Empathy Builder empowers everybody to begin an international dialogue. It enables learning and resource sharing and makes for more empathic and knowledgeable citizens of the planet without the distortions of media, propaganda, or agendas of special interest groups.

I wish Jaden Hayes would be a team member on architecting such a service. Another person I'd love to be on such a team is Roman Krznaric, author of *Empathy, Why It Matters, and How to Get It*. He and other empathetic people, along with support of social investors using crowd funding platform Indiegogo, are launching the world's first Empathy Museum in London.[4] They might be the impossipreneurs that make Empathy Builder fully take flight. I hope so.

Some people say that the world is shrinking.
I say the world is finite, we become larger.

Once our world view has been sufficiently sharpened we may feel a bit unsettled and find that our daily routine no longer satisfies. When people yearn to solve problems and explore opportunities then those desires should be met with guidance, camaraderie, and resources.

Make Meaning Department. Every person on the planet, irrespective of skills, training, experience, or socio-economic status should be able to make meaning. This includes the retired, the young, those in school, the unemployed, the fully employed, and those with temporary or permanent impairments to their normal human abilities.

The Make Meaning Department is where a person goes when they aspire to do more, when they want access to opportunities to develop their full potential, but they need a little help. This is the department whose aim is to help people reach their destination no matter if that destination is as a public servant, school teacher, tradesman, doctor, engineer, scientist, painter, babysitter, volunteer at a nonprofit, writer, or most anything else. It can be about any job, career, or vocation. But, it can also be about a hobby, skill building, or simply making human connection. If a senior citizen wants to learn about geology, the Make

Meaning Department accommodates. Think of it as humans helping humans. And if that senior's granddaughter wants to know what it's like to serve on a nonprofit board or build a software program then there is assistance for that, too. The Make Meaning Department is not exclusive; it is there to serve anybody who desires to use it.

The location for the Make Meaning Department is everywhere. While there would be physical locations where you can meet people and access resources, there would also be a global network of online resources and personnel accessible through phone, chat, video, email, etc.

With the Make Meaning Department there isn't the need for the unemployment office as we know it. We no longer need or benefit from people policing unemployment benefits. What we need is people helping people to make meaning. Since employment and enjoyment becomes a national priority of each nation, the Make Meaning Department works with people no matter their employment status.

Think of it this way, a theoretical physicists, a diplomat, and a philosopher walk into the bar. Ah, your waiting for the punchline. But, instead of a punchline I'll let you imagine the conversation that would ensue from what they've each already said on the subject.

"However difficult life may seem, there is always something you can do and succeed at."
"Work gives you meaning and purpose and life is empty without it."

Stephen William Hawking
Theoretical physicist,
cosmologist, author
(born 8 January 1942)

Gregory James Olson

"Each one of us can make a difference and help create a more humane world."

Ban Ki-moon
Secretary-General of the United Nations
Born 13 June 1944

"Work keeps at bay three great evils: boredom, vice, and need."

pen name, Voltaire
Francois-Marie Arouet
Writer, historian, philosopher, polemicist
(1694–1778)

Social Safety Net for Entrepreneurs. All entrepreneurs need community. That community consists of customers, advisors, potential partners, maybe even co-founders, and employees. But, you usually don't start a new venture and have readymade customers, employees waiting, and advisors ready to part with sage advice or get further involved. No, those things take a while to build up, especially for the first time entrepreneur who might have been previously distracted with school, a job, or life. Without a community of support it's difficult to succeed. Many run out of savings and as that is depleted so is energy and motivation. Multiply the rate of decline if a marginally supportive spouse or partner is involved. Many would-be good businesses are starved of human and financial capital before they ever fully take flight. This isn't a good thing since most jobs are created by firms less than five years old. Large established firms have demonstrated themselves to be job destroyers.[5]

If we can build vaccines for diseases we cannot see, and build fabric winged airplanes that can carry us to other continents, can't we also build systems that help humans that are negatively affected by public policy, technology changes, and corporate greed? Of course we can.

The Social Safety Net for Entrepreneurs needs to include tax reform that favors young firms that are getting started and taking risks as opposed to older firms that game the system to dodge taxes and externalize costs to society.

The Social Safety Net for Entrepreneurs would also ensure health benefits. This hasn't been a problem in all developed countries, but healthcare in America has been attacked and obstructed since it was first proposed.[6]

In exchange for the safety net, entrepreneurs who benefit will enter into a social contract that includes helping other entrepreneurs and sharing their milestones and scorecard that can help to demystify the successes and failures behind new venture success.

See also: Universal Unconditional Basic Income

Lifeline. You've probably seen the television show *Who Wants to be a Millionaire*. It has aired in 160 countries in one form or another. In it, contestants, are able to request a lifeline, when they are unsure of the answer to a question. The Lifeline gives the contestant an opportunity to phone a friend or, in some variations of the game, to ask an expert. The hope of course is that someone more knowledgeable with the question at hand will provide the correct answer and the contestant's prize money will continue to grow.

In life, we should all be so lucky to have the opportunity to contact somebody more knowledgeable than us, so that we can gain that instant clarity of thought.

If you are in, or have been to New York City you might have experienced a lifeline of sorts. There, residents, business owners, and visitors can call, click or text 311 services to have their question answered. Over 100 million calls have been received by agents on topics that cover a range of city issues.[7] But, in spite of NYC 311 services being hosted by 200 customer service pros they still do not know as much as all of us.

More and more cities have created their versions of 311 information services.

The Brooklyn Public Library in New York goes even further and connects knowledge seekers with experts in their own neighborhood. The service, named BklynShare, seeks to extend the library's role as a community resource hub. The project was awarded funding through a grant by the Knight Foundation's News Challenge.[8]

But, what we really need is a system that goes beyond city borders and utilizes experts, or civic minded researchers in the locations where those people are located. A LinkedIn group doesn't care where a person resides, neither does a Facebook friends list, or tribe of Twitter followers. Lifeline intelligently routes your question to a person appropriate to answer your question, whether across the world or at the coffee shop down the street.

Unlike the game show, there is no prize money to be awarded. Participates do, however, win knowledge and clarity of thought. People and organizations that answer questions are incented and recognized for their civic participation. Some of those participants might be working within the walls of an organization, from within their homes, or at coworking spaces.

Future Coworking Spaces. C-base in Berlin, Germany was one of the first coworking spaces in the world. Though established in 1995, by the year 2002, at a time when many were not on the Internet, a time before streaming music or movies, when Google was 4 years old and Facebook was not yet born, C-base was providing programmers with a physical location to meet and work. They made WIFI networks available and promoted free public access to the Internet. Though C-base looks like an early community oriented coworking space, the term wasn't actually coined until 1999 by Bernard De Koven, a game designer, author, and fun theorist.[9]

Today there are two camps of coworking: community oriented coworking spaces; and real estate oriented companies that wish to cash in on the millions of people who have been displaced from ordinary offices in a structurally changed world of work. With more freelancers, contractors, consultants, and even remote employees than at any time in history, the growth in coworking spaces is only destined to increase.

A big change ahead for coworking spaces includes public and private sponsorship and scholarship for some residents. It is already happening in Paris, France. In the latest round of participatory budgeting in Paris, citizens have democratically voted to spend part of the public budget on coworking spaces for young entrepreneurs.[10] It is part of their aim to become a more collaborative city.

Just as some people in 34,000 cities in 190 countries have opened up their homes to rent out lodging via Airbnb, more people will open up their home offices to share with others. Homeowners with extra space in their home offices seek the same water-cooler conversations and camaraderie that coworking residents seek and they too, seek it away from coffee shops and other distracting places. Future home construction and remodeling plans will increasingly feature such spaces from socially minded homeowners.

Though coworking spaces are known for popup impromptu brainstorming and collaboration, more and more coworking spaces will host human catalysts who are available like university professors who hold office hours.

Entrepreneurs who are good at their core offering, are often terrible at sales, marketing, and business development, unless of course those skills are their core offering. Many would rather have a job where departments would take care of those aspects of the operation. But, more and more reluctant entrepreneurs, both former employees and new graduates alike, are thrust into being business owners as corporate short-termism keep payrolls lean.

Reluctant entrepreneurs will find value in services that connect them to customers and perform aspects of their business they don't have the time, nor talent for. In the past professionals offering such services had little incentive to help budding entrepreneurs. For one, new ventures are seldom flush with cash. And secondly, in the past it has been expected by coworking space owners that such helpful talent would rent space alongside those they intend to help. Many new ventures and ideas have become stuck at this point. Coworking spaces of the future will feature catalyst talent, but it won't be on the entrepreneurs payroll, nor will it cost the coworking space owner any money. Services will be seen as beneficial to job creation and growth and as such will be invested in by the public through participatory budgeting funds and also directly through government funded programs. Corporate leaders with long term thinking will also sponsor talent and programs within coworking spaces as a continued source of innovation and an eye toward building networks of collaboration.

See also: Make Meaning Department

As technology increasingly shrinks our world we have the potential to become a global human network of talent. Large multinational corporations have long enjoyed the advantage of scale and presence in multiple locations. Governments too, have long experienced presence in other nations through the establishment of embassies and consulates. But, this isn't true of solopreneurs and small businesses who have limited physical access and resources. This is a problem because on average solopreneurs and small businesses are on the rise while older established firms continue to shed jobs and are reticent to add employees to the payroll.

As I talk about in *The Experience Design Blueprint*, the world of work has changed and it's not coming back as we knew it. Workers now have more assignments throughout their working lives than ever before and many of those assignments are being performed in a temporary capacity other than as an employee. At the same time, more employers are increasingly dependent on people who are not employees of the firm, today and in the future. This is true, whether the organization is a for-profit enterprise, nonprofit, or government. Welcome to the gig economy.[11]

There have been great inefficiencies in matching talent with available assignments. Employers cite lack of appropriate talent. But, appropriate talent cites broken experiences and too few jobs.[12]

The Innovation Clearinghouse is an omniscient system that knows the interests and capabilities of the people who make up the workforce. It works hand in hand with the Make Meaning department and it allows people to self report their current employment status, areas of interest, and locations they are willing to work.

If a person is employed full-time but has the capacity and desire to take on an additional project be it plumbing, bridge design, solar panel installation, trail building, eldercare, or anything else, the system enables people to report that desire. It also tracks certifications, qualifications, and ratings.

Organizations of any type or even people who desire assistance can access the system and request human resources. They too have a rating system. The Innovation Clearinghouse handles compensation so the people and organizations involved can focus on value creating activities and not get hung up on contracts and administration. There are plenty of problems to solve and opportunities to explore in our world.

The Innovation Clearinghouse provides technology and

personnel to nations and initiatives that need them. This has the promise to turn developing nations into developed nations. The only thing that separates the two is greed and will. The Innovation Clearinghouse is also a resource for developed nations and organizations within them that find themselves short of talent or technology.

The Innovation Clearinghouse goes beyond relief efforts and focuses on capacity building, sustainability, and progress. It is about solving problems like establishing or upgrading infrastructure, but it is also about exploring opportunities in domestic manufacturing and innovating healthcare, education, agriculture, energy and even government itself.

Most people want to make meaning, especially those who diligently went to school to learn a trade or profession. They don't want to collect unemployment, sit on the sidelines and not participate in something larger than themselves. And if their country of origin cannot put them to use today, they'd like the option to work elsewhere without fussing with work visa and immigration policies. Think of the possibilities across industries to put talent to good work. The Innovation Clearinghouse gives individuals the opportunity to be included in a world economy that is forging ahead; nobody gets left behind.

There are four analogues to learn from in building the Innovation Clearinghouse. For that we'll look to doctors, engineers, a social investor, and even an entire country.

One organization, Medecins sans Frontieres (MSF), or Doctors Without Borders, has been extremely good at mobilizing a medical strike force to respond to emergencies anywhere in the world, whether from famine, conflict, or natural disasters.

From its inception in 1971, MSF faced a series of humanitarian crises, from an earthquake in Nicaraguan capital Managua that destroyed much of the city and killed between 10,000 and 30,000 people, Cambodian refugees in

Thailand seeking sanctuary from Pol Pot's oppressive rule, to genocide in Rwanda, to famine in Ethiopia, and war in the former Yugoslavia.[13]

Nothing has changed over their history and MSF still does a remarkable job. On the day I write this an MSF mobile medical team is treating civil war refugees and economic migrants who are attempting to cross the border between Greece and Macedonia in hopes of reaching more prosperous northern European countries. Instead of being treated as refugees and offering them international protection, Macedonian border troops have "welcomed" these refugees with stun grenades and tear gas, treating them like rioters.[14][15]

Whereas Doctors Without Borders has been reactionary, the Innovation Clearinghouse is proactive. Case in point: One of my colleagues, a retired designer of outdoor gear and garments, has an innovative protective suit design to safeguard healthcare workers from the dangers of Ebola. But, as a retired person without a company or employer, this design and talent is wasted, sitting idle, never to benefit humanity.

The Innovation Clearinghouse organizes and formalizes sharing of technology and personnel no matter their location or employment status. Just as a military soldier is dispatched on orders without having to purchase an airline ticket, individuals participating in the Innovation Clearinghouse would be dispatched to a location and project where their skills and interest are a good match. Depending upon the nature of the assignment they may also work from the comfort of their home office. With the Innovation Clearinghouse my colleague's innovative suit would be put to the test and he would be engaged in solution finding activities.

The "Without Borders" notion has expanded to include many other professions.[16] Engineers Without Borders (EWB) partners with disadvantaged communities to improve their quality of life through education and implementation of sustainable engineering projects, while promoting global experience for engineers, engineering students, and similarly motivated non-engineers. EWB creates links between like-minded organizations and cuts across national borders. EWB international members work on a variety of alternative energy projects, water distribution, sanitation and pumping stations, sustainable agriculture, education and empowerment, and building shelters using sustainable local materials.[17] Because EWB projects rely on student volunteers projects can take many years and trips involving various groups of students to complete. As an example, one water project in Uganda began in 2009. In spite of eleven trips by students the project has yet to complete.

Aside from lacking the necessary engineering skills in the local community to develop the system and see it to completion, the EWB group is also held up by a lack of funds. This, in spite of the necessity of water for life and the fact that children are walking two miles to fetch unsanitary water each day. The EWB group has a local supplier for the pump and generator; they are now waiting for funds, which will come from a variety of sources such as grants from the university, personal donations, corporate sponsors, and their partner non-governmental organization (NGO).[18]

When there is the will for change and the resources to back it up, progress can happen quickly. This is especially true when the problems to be solved have readymade and knowable solutions.

Compare the slow progress of the Uganda water project to the rapid progress made when a bridge on a major interstate in Washington State was struck by a truck carrying an oversized load.

The collision caused part of the bridge span to collapse and sent cars into the river below. Traffic was immediately rerouted and a temporary bridge span was built and put in place within 27 days. Within four months a new permanent Skagit River Bridge reopened.[19]

The difference between the two projects is priority. The Burlington Mayor feared collapse of the local economy. Washington State Governor Jay Inslee declared an economic "state of emergency" for three surrounding counties in order to cope with disruption to traffic and the local economy.[20]

Thankfully, the bridge repair and replacement didn't rely on volunteers and nonprofit fundraising efforts. The Innovation Clearinghouse treats problems and opportunities such as water, sanitation, healthcare, energy, etc. as seriously as a collapsed bridge because they are as serious. Entire villages, communities, and even nations are waiting and wanting to join the ranks of developed nations if only given the chance.

Another organization to model that gives people that chance is social investor and financial cooperative, Oikocredit International.

The idea of Oikocredit began in a 1968 meeting of the World Council of Churches. Politically engaged church members from a variety of denominations began calling for an ethical investment channel that supported peace and universal brotherhood. This concept was innovative and controversial. At the time the world wrestled with issues including South Africa's Apartheid and the Vietnam War.[21]

From the onset Oikocredit believed in empowering people to help themselves. The initial organization continued to evolve eventually becoming legally incorporated in The Netherlands as Oikocredit in 1975. Oikocredit provides access to credit to empower people to invest in themselves and their future. Investment areas include microfinance, fair trade, agriculture, and renewable energy. Today, 40 years later, Oikocredit has impacted the lives of over tens of millions of people through 100's of project partners in over 70 countries.

But, it isn't enough to meet the needs of the people on the planet. Though Oikocredit has centralized staff and regional offices they still largely rely on volunteers in Support Associations and of course the investment and donations of socially minded individuals and institutions (mostly churches). Imagine a similar fully funded and resourced initiative. Instead of 10's of millions positively impacted, the number could be the seven billion humans sharing the planet. Given the opportunity, most citizens of the planet would support their tax money going toward humanitarian issues and advancing human progress. We'll revisit that notion in Participatory Budgeting.

We can learn from the various guest worker programs in place in many countries. In particular, in the Philippines, 10 percent of the population work overseas. It is a collective enterprise where the Filipino state and the individual have a big investment. It is economically vital and part of the culture. The government calls overseas workers modern heroes.[22] The Philippine Overseas Employment Administration is the government agency devoted to optimizing the benefits of the country's overseas employment program.[23] But, the system is not without problems. Many people leave children behind to earn a living. There is no global coordination of workers. Although the Philippines have reported increased Gross Domestic Product (GDP) as a result of overseas workers, there has been no real prosperity for many of the people performing the work. These workers often become trapped in permanent temporary work and are subject to the shocks of the global economy. Aside from the huge social costs, some workers report being exploited and abused.[24]

The Innovation Clearinghouse protects workers from becoming exploited and abused. It adopts and enforces International Labor Organization (ILO) standards which aim to improve the rights, livelihoods, security, and opportunities of people, families and communities around the world.[25] Workers of any skill, experience level, and country of origin who experience abusive conditions have access to safe shelter, emergency contact and justice without fear of reprisal, false charges, or other abuses. The collective nature of the Innovation Clearinghouse means that any individual employer abusing the system is up against a world collective that is focused on advancing human prosperity. The employer abusing the system will lose time and again.

The Innovation Clearinghouse, in learning from other organizations and countries, can replicate the bright spots of what is working well while safeguarding humanity from what is not. The previous scale and achievements of governments and large corporations pale in comparison to what a world body of concerned and collaborative global citizens can accomplish. No government or corporation will want to be left behind in the global innovation neighborhood.

If no government or existing organization is exploring a particular opportunity an individual can initiate a project knowing that The Innovation Clearinghouse will further identify financial and human resources who wish to contribute talent and funding.

Participatory Budgeting. Participatory Budgeting, or PB, is a democratic process in which community members directly decide how to spend part of a public budget. Here is roughly how it works:

1. Residents brainstorm ideas
2. Proposals are developed from those ideas
3. Residents vote on proposals
4. The ones with the most votes win funding

It is a bit like using Kickstarter or another crowdfunding platform, but you work directly with your neighbors and instead of using your credit card you use public money.

So what's the big deal? Why does PB matter? Well, in an era where so much wealth and power are concentrated, participatory budgeting is important:

- It can restore trust and increase government transparency
- It gets youth involved in the workings of government and the democratic process
- It increases civic participation for youth and adults alike
- It can reduce voter apathy

But, it goes beyond that. PB can actually take the guesswork out of governing. Innovation in government services and programs shouldn't be top down. They should be informed by the collective intelligence and participation of the communities they serve. PB also improves governance at the local level. In short, Participatory Budgeting helps to create more meaningful and inclusive democracies.

Participatory Budgeting has been used for cities, states, counties, schools and community organizations, and public housing. Funds have been set aside for capital projects as well as for services and programs. There are now over 1500 Participatory Budgeting processes in the world. But, there needs to be many more.

Imagine a civic engagement platform where every neighborhood was able to share their priorities so that government representatives would understand the priorities of the people they represent. PB is an important element of representative democracies and democratic regions. It is a good method to nudge ideas forward and to also nudge forward human progress.

Truth Machine Intelligence Service. Many times when it comes to economic or public policy, politicians and pundits simply echo whatever talking points fit their ideology. It isn't necessarily factual and many times benefits are overstated by proponents while the opponents use alarmist rhetoric and predictions. The Truth Machine Intelligence Service would be an intelligent system available to the public that would remove rhetoric and use science, not emotion, to predict the most certain outcome and variations.

The system would also show cause and effect as well as the related ripple effect of certain decisions made. Using such a system could help policy makers and the public better understand the relative merits of competing solutions.

For example, to alleviate traffic congestion, one solution could be to build more roads whereas another solution might be to stagger the hours of businesses and their workers. Without such a Truth Machine Intelligence Service in place, proposing a "more roads" solutions will likely be supported by those who benefit from construction either directly or indirectly.

The "stagger the hours" solution might be a superior solution but its campaign also might be underfunded and reach fewer people. The "more roads" campaign would almost certainly win. Truth Machine would provide a more objective and balanced view of the solutions so that an informed populace would make more intelligent decisions that benefit everybody. The Omniscient Truth Machine Intelligence Services sees all.

Will more people die if we stop doing bridge and road maintenance? Will there be more sickness if we allow the injection of unknown fracking chemicals into our aquifers? Are GMO crops saving the world from starvation as promised? Are the unemployed simply lazy and unskilled? Which corporations are parasites internalizing profits and earnings while externalizing human and environment costs to society.

Universal Unconditional Basic Income. Individuals have been participating in a sharing economy since before that term was invented. Collaborative networks and structures of various arrangements have also been in use for workers of all types. However, unless there are clear boundaries, expectations, and compensation they do suffer from volunteer burnout and waning interest.

In the early phases of unfunded startups and other initiatives it isn't practical to put in place formal structures around compensation. After all, they are not funded; there simply isn't any money. Many would-be great ideas and entrepreneurial ventures fizzle out as the implied financial gain isn't as compelling as actual pay that can secure food and shelter and other life's necessities. Inspiration has expiration especially when it gets in the way of putting food on the table. Universal Basic Income solves this problem. If more entrepreneurs had a basic income to rely on then the rate of success would increase and society would feel the benefits of those ventures' products and services.

Additionally, free markets have failed to address pressing social problems. This has been the domain of nonprofits, though they have endured with mixed success. Nonprofits of all types rely on volunteers. Without remuneration most volunteers must eventually cut their time short to focus on work that provides remuneration. This limits the potential of the nonprofit and shortchanges whatever social cause that nonprofit is focused on.

Whether they are entrepreneurs, a caregiver of a child or parent, or any other member of society, UBI frees humans from the demands of meeting the lower elements of Maslow's hierarchy of needs. UBI is specifically designed to provide all residents of the planet with enough to meet basic needs in their region. It stops poverty dead in its tracks. It frees humans to focus on higher order needs such as esteem and belonging that go numb when people can't meet physiological and safety needs of basic food and shelter. All countries will benefit when decreasing global poverty becomes a priority in the world.[26] It is more stable for democracies and produces more customers, more entrepreneurs, and more social good.

If you have a strong aversion to Universal Basic Income then you must ask yourself why? Is it because you work and think others should too, out of fairness? Do you think that it cannot be paid for or that we'd all become slackers and society would collapse? If it is the former, then consider why not put babies, puppies and old people to work.

I'd like to share with you a recent experiment that shows great promise. It actually busted every single prediction made by economists. Keep in mind the economists' opinions were based on ideology and patterns of belief, whereas the experiment produced real data based on real people in real villages.

Here is how it worked. The experiment was based in rural India over an 18 month period from 2011-2013. It involved 12,000 people in 20 villages. It also included a control group from which to compare village outcomes.

This was the first such experiment in Indian history. It was determined that in the villages the average family needed the equivalent of $24/month to cover basic needs. The program was universal; funds went to every human being, including children. Each adult received 300 rupees and each child 150, paid to the mother or guardian. Money received was unconditional. It wasn't means tested and there were absolutely no conditions. Funds bypassed middlemen and went directly into the hands of the recipient, for the first couple of months in cash and later electronically to a bank account.[27] Here is what the best economists in the world predicted would happen.

Predictions
- It would be difficult to adopt
- There would be major problems opening bank

accounts

- There would be no incentive to work, resulting in decreased labor
- Money would go to waste. It would got to prostitutes, tobacco and social ills.
- It simply cost too much

Now, see what actually happened based on real data with real human beings in the villages.

Implementation and Financial Inclusion

- Take-up on the program was rapid with 93% receiving grants in cash form in the first month
- Very few reported having issues setting up bank accounts. After a couple of months there were no issues. Also, bank accounts were opened by cooperatives controlled by the people.
- Savings increased and households began using their accounts for saving, rather than keeping money at home

Housing and Sanitation

- Recipients of basic income grants were significantly more likely to make improvement to their dwellings
- Main improvement were to walls, and roofs, and latrines
- Many switched to better drinking water sources, energy sources for cooking, and lighting

Nutrition and Diet

- There were improvement in children weight-for-age, it was even more pronounced with girls since boys in rural India were already favored
- Cash grant recipients were significantly more likely to have enough income for their daily food needs
- More varied diets with greater relative consumption of

fruits and vegetables
- Were not more likely than others to increase spending on "private bads" such as alcohol or tobacco

Health and Healthcare
- Cash grant households reported a lower incidence of common illnesses
- More regular treatment and more regular taking of medicines
- Increased spending on medical treatment

Impact on the Disabled
- Those with disabilities had more access to food and to medical assistance
- Household members with disabilities had greater voice in how money was spent
- Some disabled became economically active, overcoming constraints to their full membership in village society

Schooling
- Enrollment rates of children from 4 to 18 years was 12% higher in the cash transfer villages
- Transfers led to increased spending on essentials for school, including stationery, shoes, uniforms and basic equipment
- Cash grants were associated with more regular school attendance, with 29% of cash transfer households reporting an improvement, compared with 13% in control villages
- Increased spending on transportation to school

Economic Activity, Work and Production
- Increased labor, productivity and more people were working

- Cash grant householder were twice as likely to have increased their production work as non-transfer households
- Purchased more livestock to increased production
- Many families used cash grants to buy small items for production
- More likely to increase their income from work in spite of it being a difficult year due to weather conditions
- Three time as likely to start a new business or production activity as others, with a majority attributing that to the cash grants

Debt and Savings

- Severe indebtedness was found in over three-quarters of all households
- Cash grants were associated with a significant reduction in indebtedness, both because recipients used the money to reduce existing debt and because they used the money to avoid going into further debt. Those receiving cash grants were more than twice as likely to reduce debt

The results of the unconditional basic income experiment were essentially the opposite of what economists predicted. All social indicators were better and it is worth mentioning again, this was based on real data with real human beings. Extrapolating the experiment to other areas can be potentially transformative for the people in the regions affected and their trading partners.

UBI is important in developing nations but is it equally important in developed nations. The world of work has structurally changed. Large percentages of the population, if they are working at all, are working in a gig economy, leaving them with income insecurity. Technology evolution and corporate behaviors are colluding to speed the rate of job obsolescence (jobsolescence) and joblessness. This does not bode well for an economy that relies on demand from customers (actually human beings with money to spend) for products and services. Jobs of all sorts are going away at a faster rate than what new ones are appearing.

With UBI, people have an income to fall back on so they can keep from slipping into poverty and in-between or alongside work assignments they can pursue projects, create ventures, pool resources, and explore their capabilities by plugging into the Make Meaning Department and the Innovation Clearinghouse. UBI is good for individuals and it is good for human progress. Perhaps that is why concerned citizens and some policy makers in many countries are moving the subject along.

Successful trials have been run in Canada and Namibia. But, in true impossipreneur fashion further expansion is encountering harsh resistance by politicians.

Likewise citizens in Switzerland gathered enough signatures on an initiative for unconditional basic income to trigger a nationwide referendum on it. The Swiss Federal Council rejected the referendum citing concerns just as economist had earlier predicted about the experiment in India. It doesn't matter, a people's initiative bypasses the government and goes directly to the people even against the ruling government's wishes.[28]

Other countries where basic income is getting movement includes Denmark, The Netherlands, Finland, and France. Though not unconditional, universal basic income has been in place in Brazil since 2004 and has dramatically reduced poverty. Though the program was denounced for encouraging laziness, the World Bank found that the program did not discourage working, and actually encouraged harder work and entrepreneurship.[29]

One of the longest standing experiments in basic income is the Alaska Permanent Fund Dividend, established in 1976 to provide a means of conserving a portion of the state's revenue from mineral resource to benefit all generations of Alaskans.[30] Although the dividend, paid annually in October, isn't enough to meet basic needs, it has been found to be helpful to residents in servicing debt, increasing savings, making large purchases, and meeting ordinary expenses. It is also attributable for increasing demand in the state's businesses and attracting more people to the state for jobs.[31]

Politicians and economists can be dead wrong. Critics and opponents were wrong in Alaska, they were wrong in India, and they'll probably be wrong wherever basic income is attempted next. Perhaps a key learning here is don't let your ideology blind you to reality.

> **"Don't get so set on your goal**
> **that you lose your humanity."**
> *Cicero*
> *Roman author,*
> *orator, politician*
> *(106 BC–43 BC)*

Subsidizing consumption alleviates poverty, but it does not interrupt capitalism's incessant consolidation of wealth.

For that we'll need other societal safeguards, for people, communities and the environment. We can either create new economic models or create a patchwork of fixes when things are not trending in a desirable direction.

In this chapter I've shared ideas to create a more inclusive society that empowers individuals to reach their potential and to achieve social well being.

I've also provided ideas related to confronting reality, whether that is about a particular issue or understanding the perspectives of others.

There is no shortage of opportunities to explore and problems to solve in the world, which is why I advocate a global innovation network that people can plug into, whether in their own neighborhood or across the world. All of this, combined with participatory budgeting will create a more engaged and civil society. It will also increase the stability of democracies as they become more responsive to the people who comprise those democracies.

But, all of this will be for not, if we don't rein in the abuse and insatiable appetite of corporations that wish to grow without bound, while they privatize profits and socialize losses. The people within those corporations, especially the leadership, seem to work above the law, in the shadows, without regard for the environment, human beings, or even the long term health of the organizations they "lead."

It is time we intentionally design the world we wish to live in. That world does not include economic shocks, massive inequality, extreme poverty with no path to escape, short-termism, environmental ruin, and marginalized people.

Revisiting the Corporation. First off, the idea that a corporation has only a duty to its shareholders is malarkey. It shows anemic thinking. Imagine you were hosting a birthday party and only paid heed to the person having the birthday. You'd be in trouble from the start. The guests' experiences matter too, right? After all, if there were no guests, or guests left the party prematurely, the party would surely feel different. There would be less singing, fewer gifts to open, and too much cake to consume. Worse yet, if there were any activities or games planned these would have far fewer participants. In the end, the person having the birthday party would also have a diminished experience and ultimately be disappointed.

Corporations share some of the same characteristics as parties. Like a party host, a corporation has many stakeholders, not just the guest of honor. And, each of those stakeholders has expectations, whether the corporation has made explicit promises or they are merely implied. Also, like the party, when some of those stakeholders become unhappy, it can ultimately bring disappointment to shareholders. Early signs might include lost customers, disengaged employees, and reluctant partners. Left uncorrected the corporation experiences a loss of competitive position in the marketplace. At its worse, it could mean legal actions, environmental ruin, and even outright failure.

Metrics that Matter. Imagine if our collective human metric was to be happier. What if organizations of all types were to forget about growth at all costs, or cutting costs beyond expectations and all reasonableness? What if executive focus and accountability included more than earnings and profits? What if share price wasn't the most important metric?

Imagine a world where alleviating suffering or maximizing happiness mattered. If an organization had big profits, but miserable employees, unhappy customers, or wreaked havoc on the environment, then this would be made visible; it would mean something.

In this possible world the focus would be, "Are we making our stakeholders happy?" Imagine the possibilities for employee and civic engagement, education, health, community building, and human progress. Happy customers would be the norm.

We would collectively focus on making customers happy and treating them with respect like some thoughtful companies do today. As a result we would be more prosperous, tolerant, less polarized, compassionate, and maybe even peaceful. Is it possible?

I think it is our duty as the dominant species on the planet and chief stewards of our shared environment to find out.

If you're in agreement with this thinking that new metrics are needed, then know that you and I are not alone.

On July 19, 2011, the United Nations General Assembly adopted U.N. Resolution 65/309 wherein among other things they stated the pursuit of happiness as a fundamental human goal and recognized that the gross domestic product indicator was not designed to and does not adequately reflect the happiness and well-being of people in a country.

It turns out that GDP and corporate profits can be up and to the right, while at the same time, those that helped it get that way may experience personal decline in terms of real wages, household wealth, and overall prosperity.

Example: GargantuaCorp. As an extreme fictitious example, consider GargantuaCorp that manufactures most all of the goods within a country. In order to achieve this, it employs contractors for meager wages with no benefits and uses a bank of slaves that receive much needed experience in lieu of pay. The output of GargantuaCorp is incredible since there are few other alternative companies to work for. GargantuaCorp provides nearly all of the food, equipment, transportation, and household goods that society needs. GargantuaCorp also provides banking and debt services so that "employees" can afford to purchase the goods they help to create. In terms of GDP, the nation hosting GargantuaCorp is deemed to be doing fabulously well. Each year, GDP is up and to the right and profits are handsome. Some politicians and investors consider GargantuaCorp to be a darling. But, there is a darker, more sinister side to the story. Society is in decline. Poverty has increased, many who wish to work or make meaning cannot, wealth inequality is more lopsided than during feudal times, and the environment is suffering in the name of progress.

Metrics lie and distort reality. Recessions measure consecutive quarters of decline in GDP. There is no real measure for the happiness of a nation, only their combined economic output. Even the U.S. Misery Index initiated under President Lyndon Johnson is limited to inflation and unemployment.

Ignoring this reality traps our thinking, our public policies, and our human progress.

Example: Oikocredit International ESG Scorecard In my work as a volunteer board member for Oikocredit Northwest, a support association for global social investor Oikocredit International, I've become aware of their Environmental, Social, and Governance (ESG) Scorecard. Since Oikocredit International does its work in seventy plus countries through hundreds of partners, it is essential to have social performance criteria in place to screen, vet, and manage partners.

The ESG Scorecard helps Oikocredit field staff understand partner organizations in terms of environmental impact, outreach and targeting efforts, client benefit and welfare, governance, and responsibility to its community and staff. Oikocredit International is concerned with a balance between social and financial viability. It's internally developed ESG Scorecard sets quantitative standards by which to measure and evaluate potential partners.

Oikocredit isn't a Wall Street Darling, but it is a social darling. Investing in people is the tagline and it isn't lip service. Can you name a Fortune 500 Company that "invests in people" and leads the way in social performance? I cannot.

Humanity would be better served if more companies operated with social performance objectives. Because they don't, and this book is a hopeful journey through tomorrow — for all people, not solely the corporation — we'll have to enact a few measures. We'll start with measures, actually. First up, an unlikely measure.

Household Prosperity Index. This index shows how individuals households and their occupants are doing across a range of measures financial and otherwise. We need public policies that help move that very important metric up and to the right.

Parasitic Index. This measure shows how much a corporation leeches off of society's infrastructure and labor force as compared to the prosperity of that labor force and the communities they call home.

Profit Arrestor. Idle Capital Arrestor. When profits continue to accumulate and the corporate begins hoarding cash, it is time for that corporation to become reacquainted with innovation and investing in progress. One related and alarming signal is when corporations engage in stock buybacks, which create no real value for a company or its stakeholders.

Tax Fairness. There is no free lunch, that is unless you are a corporation. It's even better when you have a big lobbying machine to work politicians to your advantage, to the disadvantage and dismay of citizens.

Let's make visible the taxes corporation actually pay, especially multinationals that play country off of country, all the while hiding profits in tax havens. In the future, this ends. There is no free lunch for corporate giants.

Revoke the Charter of the Corporation. Taken together these measures indicate the wholesomeness of a corporation and its ability to serve its many stakeholders. When that stops happening, then the corporation needs to be pared down, taken apart, and in some cases the corporate charter needs to be revoked.

How Big it Too Big? Imagine a reservoir of water behind

a dam. A dam that never opens, starving all vegetation and life downstream of the water. The water is stacked ever higher. The mountainous reservoir is reinforced with concrete, and built higher and higher so it can contain more and more water. But why? Exactly. There is no good answer. Bigger is not better at all costs.

Just as Ronald Reagan said, "Mr. Gorbachev, tear down this wall," it is now time to say, "Corporate giants with poor measures, it's time to pare down the walls that divide you and humanity. You are on the wrong side of history."

Chapter Summary

It's hard to imagine having the freedoms and social progress without serious attention paid to wealth and economy for all people on the planet.

Since the Industrial Revolution, the land elites were joined by those who became titans of industry. Little has changed. But, I don't believe our mindset to be fixed like our eye color. We can do better.

We must do better because we need people to have social mobility in this world. The next Albert Einstein or Max Planck or Elon Musk or Mahatma Gandhi might be a child denied nutrition, education, and other social innovations that many in developed nations take for granted. That child might be in a developing nation or the developed nations, in a city, right around the corner from you.

Social mobility should be within the reach of every human being on the planet. If you think otherwise, ask yourself why you feel that way?

The pursuit of happiness is a fundamental human goal. The United Nations has adopted a resolution to that effect. And, the founding fathers of the United States of America believed in the pursuit of happiness so much they wrote it into the constitution. They knew what it was like to live under oppressive political and corporate rule. Setting up in

America was a rejection of both.

Let's not return to the past. It wasn't that great for most people. Let's have a reset. Let's have a rebirth, a new renaissance, a new progressive era and let's believe that we can change our minds and those around us, giving social mobility to people just as we have given them the mobile phone.

In the next chapter we'll revisit mobility in a different sense. As mentioned in the introduction, carry systems were some of the first systems invented by people.

6 TRANSPORTATION

Humans have long been fascinated with transportation, or is it transport? Ah, you see those words are used interchangeably today. But, in the past they had very distinct meanings. If you were a thief during 18th century England you might find yourself receiving a sentence of transportation. Huh? What?

Transport originally meant to carry across. It is Latin from *transportare* and comes from trans – "across" and portare "carry."

By contrast, the word transportation was reserved for people who were banished or forced into exile. The practice dates to Roman times and was popularized under English Law. Criminals condemned to transportation found themselves becoming residents of the British Colonies far away from London. The first destination was America. But after the American Revolution ended in 1783 the newly formed United States refused to accept any more convicts. Botany Bay in Australia became the new destination.

How did this evolve? At one time in England there were 222 crimes that were punishable by death, among them stealing, cutting down a tree, and robbing a rabbit warren.[1] Some thought capital punishment too severe leading to the passage by British Parliament of The Transportation Act 1717. The goal of getting rid of the criminals was still accomplished, but they were no longer killed.

Transportation was expensive. The overhead required to move the first 1000 prisoners on six ships to Botany Bay was four additional ships. A 1720 extension to the Act, authorized the state to make payments to contracted merchants.[2]

Though ships were the de facto mode of transportation, people of the industrial era were probably already dreaming of next generation modes of transport. No doubt you've thought of this next one. This idea seems to have many founders and has been popularized in science fiction. One of the earliest documented findings is an 1878 paper that made reference to The Latest Wonder, the teleport.[3]

Teleportation. This age old desire has you appearing instantaneously in one location while you vanish in another. Or, put another way you arrive without traveling. No Transportation Security Administration (TSA)? Well then, sign me up!

Think of it this way, you push a button and poof (okay maybe that is the wrong sound) voila – you're gone. Or, are you? Your atoms and bits circulate as you are "beamed" to another location. Only question is should you warn others that you're on your way? Maybe ding dong, and milliseconds later, you warn others, "I've arrived."

There have been some developments in teleportation using photons and entangled atoms. Entanglement is the unusual behavior of elementary particles where they become linked, acquiring a merged identity. So, when something happens to one, something happens to the other; no matter how far apart they are.

It is interesting and has ramifications for quantum

computing and secure communications that can't be hacked or eavesdropped (sorry NSA).

For now, the movement of people pursuing teleportation is still plainly in the impossipreneur category for a couple of reasons. First, we'd have to overcome the massive amounts of information that would need to be represented. After all the human body is made up of seven billion billion billion atoms.[4]

But, that's the small number. The laws of physics say that any atom of carbon is identical to any other atom of carbon. So, if you'd like to reappear as a human and not, say a tree, we would have to actually communicate the states of those atoms. The particular arrangement of an atom's electrons, or protons, or neutrons is what makes it special. So, an already impossibly large computing problem just got massively bigger.

But, there is a second reason Teleportation is in the impossipreneur category. Even if we could overcome the computing problem we still face the quantum mechanics measurement problem. Namely, in determining the arrangement of subatomic particles inside the atom we would necessarily influence those particles.[5] Poof — back to the drawing board.

Even when we do overcome those reasons we'll undoubtedly face the next obstacle, a lack of willing volunteers. The first experiments gone wrong could lead to some pretty gooey and disturbing images. Instead of telling stories of children who died chasing balls into the street (which my great aunt did at age 10. R.I.P. Aunt Annie) we'll be telling stories of our risky relatives who tempted fate in a teleporter.

Or, another approach to recruiting teleport volunteers is return to the modern day equivalent of the Transportation Act. Teleport those convicts to…. I didn't say it, you were thinking it!

Some of the earliest designed transport systems were carry systems not for prisoners or even people, but for food. First to eat it and eventually to discard it. Food scraps, packaging and waste have to go somewhere. In developed nations it goes to compost, a recycling station (if we are lucky), the landfill or a transfer station.

Instead of experimenting with the Teleportation of people, let's beam our garbage, teleporting it directly to the landfill. No more need to roll out the garbage cans on garbage day. Imagine freeing the landscape from the blight of dumpsters and garbage cans. Teleport it directly to where it will be broken down into its components, recycled, or composted, etc.

For developing nations the story is a little different. As developing nations expand they usually leapfrog developed nations in terms of technology; they don't follow the same adoption curve. For example, many people in developing nations gained access to the Internet, but not in the same way as developed nations where we first had a dialup modem and then eventually replaced it with faster broadband service. Developed nations, with the help of NGOs, governments, and companies that wanted to access the worlds disconnected and unbanked, pressed the fast forward button and went directly to accessing the Internet through mobile phones.[6] They further leapfrogged developed nations with an advanced mobile payment system. In developing nations such as Kenya and Uganda it is quite prevalent.[7] In that dimension they are already living a future that people in developed nations have yet to realize. The CEO of ruggedized bicycle manufacturer, World Bicycle Relief, shared with me an image of a phone screen purchase confirmation of a person in Kenya who had purchased a buffalo bike (ruggedized bicycle).[8] I've yet to see a similar purchase confirmation on a smartphone in a developed nation.

Beam the Poo. Developing nations that lack access to a sewerage system could adopt Beam the Poo technology. It would send human waste directly from a bathroom like facility (the collector station) directly to a treatment facility, skipping years of infrastructure build out that other developed cities have gone through.

Dematerializer. Extending the teleporter concept further, it would be useful to devise a version that would permit a person to "dematerialize" as necessary, either to avoid disaster or trouble, or to medically "materialize" elsewhere as necessary or desirable. This method of traveling is depicted in science fiction and also in arcade and video games as "hyperspace." Although that term literally translates as above the speed of light, a person utilizing such a device need only be faster than whatever situation is putting them in harm, e.g., the mugger or the mudslide or in the case of Aunt Annie, a moving car.

Okay, coming back to a more immediate future. It would be super to free people from harm using an intermediate technology on the way to hyperspace or the teleporter.

Modern vehicles protect their occupants using a number of safety features, including airbags. If you are a passenger in a vehicle so equipped, you remain mostly safe in the event your vehicle strikes or is struck by another vehicle or large object. It's all well and good for people inside the car. The danger still exists for those outside the car — pedestrians, bicycles, and motorcycles.

It has been shown that in areas with low bicycle density, vehicle cyclist or vehicle pedestrian collisions are higher than in areas with high bicycle density. The reason for this is the little contract your eye and brain make with one another. Simply put, you don't see what you're not looking for. Psychologist call this phenomena, inattentional blindness.[9] If a driver is expecting to see other cars and not bicycles, pedestrians, motorcycles, and scooters, then they likely won't see them. Still think you can read that map or text while driving, too? Think again. You are not smarter than your human brain.

Motorcycles Masquerading as Cars. One way to make motorcycles more likely to be seen by drivers is to make motorcycles look more like cars. Motorcyclist riding in parallel with another rider accomplishes this, but that isn't always practical . One company, Motolight, is aware of this phenomena and is producing riding lights that can be added to a motorcycle's calipers, fairing, or fenders. The lights provide more visibility, but also increase the spread between the beams, making the motorcycle appear more like the vehicle drivers expect to see.[10]

Adding dual lights to a motorcycle is a great innovation as is adding airbags inside the vehicle. But, in the event of a collision it would be great to protect the people outside the vehicle as well.

For motorcyclists and bicycles this is a already a possibility. Swedish company, Hövding, has created a compact stylish collar that can be worn around the neck by cyclists. Upon impact the airbag inflates and creates a protective collar for the head and neck. The innovative system even includes a little black box that records what happened during the accident.[11]

But, what about granny? No, I really mean that. I witnessed a vehicle-pedestrian collision one rainy afternoon in Seattle. It was terribly sad. It was a cold and dreary fall day (hey, we have nice days, too) and a little old woman (most certainly a granny) stepped off of the curb and onto the crosswalk. She probably didn't think she was in danger. With coffee in one hand and an umbrella in the other she strolled across the road, safely in the bounds of the clearly marked crosswalk.

The vision of what happened next continues to replay in my mind, which is one reason I'm sharing it here. A driver making a right hand turn drove directly into her. No doubt he was looking to his left for traffic while his car inched slowly toward the right. Not seeing any traffic to the left, he accelerated into the crosswalk where the unwitting accomplice to the crash received a direct blow. It was an unfair match, a couple of tons of steel surrounding an airbag versus not much more weight than a few bags of groceries, vulnerable, and exposed to the elements. Everything stopped, that is except for granny. Upon impact, the umbrella, the coffee, and granny all went airborne in slightly different directions, like water fanning from the top of a fountain.

While the driver may not have seen her, his car equipped with sensors most surely would have seen her. Imagine that these sensors triggered an audible alert clueing him into the changing surroundings. You may have seen similar warning systems in dense urban areas where cars exit parking garages onto the sidewalk before entering the street. There are audible warnings for both parties, "Warning vehicle approaching" and "Pedestrian Ahead."

External Airbag. But, we are dealing with imperfect humans. So, in the event the person behind the wheel does not heed the audible warning, vehicles could be equipped with an External Airbag. Granny will still be struck by the vehicle with the inattentive driver, but at least the impact will be lessened.

This is increasingly important. It turns out granny isn't alone. According to the International Traffic Safety Data and Analysis Group (IRTAD), comprised of 70 organizations from 39 countries — representing a wide range of public and private bodies with a direct interest in road safety — close to 40 percent of all pedestrians killed belong to the age group 65 plus.[12] With aging populations and the encouragement of walking as healthy active transportation, the number of seniors being struck by vehicles is on the rise.

External Airbags will become increasingly important as driverless vehicles enter the scene. It is one thing for an inattentive driver to hit you as a pedestrian. It is quite another things to be struck by a driverless vehicle, the least empathetic of all drivers. We'll have to ensure that in the event of a collision the machine doesn't simply scurry away to its next assignment. One partial solution to lessen the physical impact of a driverless car-pedestrian collision is to use a External Airbag. In fact, Google was recently awarded a patent for a pedestrian airbag. It turns out they fear negative public reaction in the event of a collision.

As driverless cars gain adoption we'll all benefit from increased communication among and beyond the cars. Traffic cameras are very limited right now. Imagine being able to see through the "eyes" of the cars in and around the area you wish to travel. Perhaps you wish to see the weather, the wait time for a bus, or the congestion you'll likely encounter for the bicycle trip you are about to make.

But, the car as an information network hub being fed by its plethora of sensors and systems can go beyond merely reconnaissance. These cars can also play a very important role as history reporters, even emergency dispatch. Cameras and sensors and algorithms don't lie. They don't misremember as humans do.

I was once a witness to a motorcycle accident where a small car made a left turn directly in the path of the motorcyclist. I was traveling in the same direction as the vehicle. I saw the car spin around after the motorcycle struck it in the side. The cyclist somersaulted through the air and landed on his back.

I gave a witness statement as did the passenger in my

vehicle. Even though my friend and I saw the same accident from the same vantage point we gave two different versions of what happened. Who was right? I wish I knew.

Had there been two driverless cars in the area, recalling what their sensors and systems had seen, recorded, and processed, there would be no such conflict.

In the future, it is much more likely that you will be struck by a vehicle with a human driver making a preventable mistake than by a driverless vehicle. If and when that does happen, I hope you'll benefit from the objective information retrieved from such a driverless information network.

This information network spanning vehicles would know more than any individual driver possibly could. Also, it would be objective and its purpose would be to educate and serve humanity without any special agenda. Unlike its human counterparts the network would also be able to recall history from the same location, potentially giving planners clues to dangerous developments and usage patterns.

Labyrinth of Omniscient Vehicle Educators (LOVE). Information retrieved could be used by an ecosystem of developers to create applications and services for many purposes including: route planning, traffic forecasting and mitigation, road repair, signal and lighting improvements, parking availability, etc. Such a people first information network could appropriately be called the Labyrinth of Omniscient Vehicle Educators (LOVE).

It is my hope that nobody ever patents such a system, that it remain open, and that such a system would be additive to any vehicle operating algorithms. After all, we don't need an army of ant cars controlled by some vicious mother queen.

A couple of side notes are in order here, one on patents and the other on innovation.

Patent or Publish?

Patents can retard progress. I would have rather Google pursue the pedestrian airbag without patenting it, in the interest of public safety.

After all, as a society, wouldn't we really want all driverless cars to have such a safety feature, not solely Google? Of course we would. This was the approach of Jonas Salk when he successively created a vaccine for Polio. He chose not to pursue a patent.[13] Or, Google could do what Elon Musk of Tesla Motors has done. On the Tesla Motors blog on June 12, 2014, Musk announced, "Tesla will not initiate patent lawsuits against anyone who, in good faith, wants to use our technology." He also shared that the patents that lined the lobby have all been removed, in the spirit of the open source movement, for the advancement of electric vehicle technology.[14]

Rather than adopting a we win-you lose mentality, I'd like to see more industry collaboration to benefit all of us. The Innovation Clearinghouse described in Chapter 5 demands it.

Will the Development of Driverless Cars be Like Smartphones and the Crash of the Walled Garden?

Innovation rarely follows existing patterns. Some of the most interesting problems and opportunities often happen at the edges of our responsibilities and lay beyond the boundaries of our organizations. They require new thinking and new conversations.

In the pre-iPhone era, before Google and Apple arrived on the mobile phone scene with the Open Handset Alliance that created Android and the iPhone respectively, mobile network operators such as Vodafone, Orange, T-Mobile, Verizon, etc. and device manufacturers such as RIM BlackBerry, Motorola,

Nokia, and Samsung provided access to their devices and networks for a relatively few number of application developers as compared to today's marketplaces. This also severely limited the choices available to consumers. At the time, executives argued that networks needed security and that application certification programs were limited in resources.

But, critics made up of consumers and organizations developing applications and services, criticized this walled garden approach; they wanted access. Access continued to be limited; the congressional-like in fighting only prompted two outsiders to ignite a new phase of the mobile phone revolution. Most recognize the trigger for this revolution as the use of touchscreen technology in devices like the iPhone, but the even larger piece was the increasingly accessible marketplace offered by first Apple and subsequently, Android. This happened because of two outsiders to the mobile device world rejected the industry imposed limitations.

Google and Apple broadened their view and changed the conversation. In doing so, they got more human and now have raised the bar for all mobile device manufacturers and mobile network operators. Many of the previous industry stalwarts continue to play catch-up to these new more human and experience-centric companies. Remember the day old bread theory? For those playing catch up, their bread may have already gone bad; for some, it may be too late.

Traditional automotive companies have much to gain by reframing what it looks like to be an automotive company in an era of driverless cars, car sharing, personal pods, etc.

There is much to gain if they participate in a changing conversation and much to lose if they cling to past ideals, just as phone manufacturers and mobile operating systems discovered in their futile attempt to protect the walled garden.

Personal Transport Pod. Several high profile companies have announced driverless or driver assisted cars. As technologically advanced as these cars are, they still are very much car-like. What if we drop the trappings of the car and think differently. Perhaps what many people really desire is a Personal Transport Pod.

First we had Segways. Then came along single wheel devices that you can stand, lean, and twist to circumnavigate various types of terrain while the electric wheel propels you forward.

Now, imagine needing to travel to the store, downtown, to the airport, work, or wherever. The weather is nice so you opt for open air, no top. But, you don't have to stand; instead you comfortably sit down. You can even carry a bag or pick one up while at the store.

Now imagine as the weather become a little pesky, you slide the glass cover over the top, as a skier riding a chairlift would lower the restraining or safety bar. The personal transport pod is perfectly suitable when traveling alone, like many do when they commute. It is much safer than a conventional motorcycle especially with dedicated lanes.

As you reach your destination or place where you change modes of transportation from pod to walking or rail or bus, you simply leave the Personal Transport Pod behind. There is no need to find parking or allow extra time. Personal Transport Pods "park" themselves and become part of the municipal transport infrastructure, much like a sidewalk or bus stop. Not only are they self parking, they are self stacking so they take up less urban footprint compared to their gas guzzling archaic predecessors.

There is no need to retrieve the personal transport pod, you don't own it. Besides, there will be another available when and where you need it. Simply call, text, or message one and you'll have the option to have it come to you or be notified where the closest one is.

But, sometimes people want to connect into a larger transport systems, like dolphins in a pod. Maybe you're feeling social or perhaps simply traveling to the same place together and need more capacity. Personal transport pods are designed to accommodate this naturally occurring behavior. Being social is natural in the animal world. It happens with dolphins, whales, crows, primates, and humans.

Personal transport pods can be ganged together, in a caravan or pod of pods. Think of it as a people train, a bit like a roller coaster, but made up of personal pods. As next generation rail, transit, and marine vessel systems evolve, they can be designed to accommodate pods as well.

There are benefits to traveling together. Long haul truckers have long realized benefits of platooning, or following together in close proximity. Done correctly, it can reduce energy consumption, improve traffic flow and improve safety.[15] Properly sized pods can be clustered in a two by x formation where x is any practical number.

Traveling together can also have social benefits. Aside from alleviating congestion, eliminating parking concerns, and saving time, by traveling in a pod you're able to socialize, relax, read, plan, or play together. This is especially true as driverless systems free us from the confines of the hands upon the wheel and eyes upon the road.

Though pods could be officially coupled, they needn't be. Like undulating birds that never collide, personal transport pods can be designed to move along, together, toward their destination without mishap. When you are nearing your destination, your personal pod can decouple from the main group, similar to a bus stopping to let passengers on or off. Except in this case, the decoupling doesn't require a full stop like a bus does, that inconveniences other passengers.

Driverless Delivery Pods and **Pod Caravans.** Large numbers of traffic accidents with fatalities involve a truck or a van. We can improve the attentiveness of delivery drivers, by replacing them with sensors, and systems. Using Driverless Delivery Pods and Pod Caravans to deliver packages makes good sense, both for safety but also to alleviate congestion. Utilizing pods during nonpeak commuting times including the evening, frees up roads for other modes of transport.

As a driverless delivery pod arrives the person expecting delivery is notified via text, email, phone or preferred method. They are given an access code and are then able to retrieve the contents being delivered. In the future a delivery assist person may travel via scooter, bike, or simply walk as they work among various delivery pods on a route, perhaps in the neighborhood they live.

Even if we don't quite have teleportation, personal winged flight, or personal transport pods we can do something to make our current vehicles safer for those inside and outside the vehicle.

Smart city leaders and transportation planners are already taking action. They ban heavy trucks in city centers, they design better intersections, and stagger traffic lighting.

But, they are not the only ones working on solutions. Manufacturers are answering the call for innovation, too.

Traffic Ahead Movie Screen. Samsung is working on a See Through Safety Truck in Argentina where statistics on traffic accidents are among the highest in the world.[16] Overtaking a large truck on a single lane highway or road can be very dangerous. Drivers cannot see what lies ahead posing a danger should they decide to pass. Instead of large slow moving vehicles creating a blind wall to drivers, those same large obstacles could be equipped with cameras mounted in the front and video displays on the rear. The view ahead of the truck can be safely passed along to the vehicles following, so that drivers can make safer informed passing decisions. Think of it as a Traffic Ahead Movie Screen.

Similar systems could be made available for other large slow moving vehicles including all tractor trailers, busses, and motor homes.

The same concept could be applied to rearview mirrors and corner beams that occlude much of the driver's view in a conventional vehicle.

Blindspot Remover. Using light shaping, camera, and projection technology the blind spots that drivers encounter can be fully eliminated. Bicycle or pedestrian accidents involving vehicles can become a thing of the past. Pedestrian and bicycles that are currently invisible to drivers due to the vehicle's fabrication can instead become images projected or otherwise reproduced in plain view for drivers. The beams that hold up the roof no longer need to block a driver's view of the fragile pedestrians and bicycles "hidden" behind them. Researchers in Japan are working on such a vehicle, the Toyota Prius see-through. Jaguar Land Rover is also working on similar see through technology that has the promise to reduce such accidents.[17]

The Oscillating See Through Rear View Mirror. This mirror allows you to see what is ahead of the vehicle, but also gives you a periodic view of what is going on behind the vehicle. Such a system would restore the view currently obstructed by large size of the rear view mirror relative to the wind screen in most modern vehicles. Forward sloping windshields reduce the visibility drivers have due to the increased relative size of the rear view mirror. Mirrors that include only rear facing camera systems ignore the fact that pedestrians, bicycles, and other objects in front of the vehicle are in apparent plain view but are de facto largely invisible to the driver. Oscillating the mirror view between front and rear vehicle images, provides the driver with increased situational awareness and improves the safety of those outside the vehicle.

You might have already leapt to the possibility of driverless cars that wouldn't care about such blind spots. You see, with driverless cars, there are no blind spots and human error. The sensors that detect objects all around the vehicle do the same function as the oscillating see through rear view mirror does when combined with human vision.

We wouldn't want the driverless cars to lack sensors or ignore any particular direction. Likewise, we don't want humans to not see in front or behind the vehicle, either.

Another human driving vulnerability is when a driver focuses their attention elsewhere for navigation help, whether that is a GPS attached to the wind screen, a smartphone application, or the old school paper map.

Ghost Car Navigation. This system promises that you'll not be distracted by the GPS screen occluding your windshield or worse the navigation screen on your smartphone. The heads-up display technology is already being testing by Jaguar Land Rover.

Drivers simply follow the ghost image as it makes turns and navigates toward the programmed destination. Since the ghost image appears in the windscreen, the driver is able to remain attentive and not get distracted inside the vehicle cockpit.

Even in a driverless car situation it will be nice to see the ghost car leading the way toward the destination.

Chapter Summary

There is much innovation and progress to be made in the area of transportation. We can and should obsolete gridlock. Along with it we'd see the disappearance of noise pollution, frustrated angry drivers, and of course blocked intersections.

One thing is certain. We need to invite new conversations. We'll need to free data. We'll need to empower others. Following the existing patterns probably won't get us to desirable outcomes. We'll need people and especially profit-centric corporations to focus on publishing and cooperating as opposed to patenting and protecting.

Let's get the Innovation Clearinghouse doing its part. People have ideas and talent; it doesn't all reside with Google X, Tesla Motors, Jaguar Land Rover, the Department of Transportation, etc. Let's give others a seat at the table. Let's change the conversation entirely. Transportation leaders don't fail when they don't deliver on transportation solutions, they fail when they don't have the right conversations that could lead to more desirable solutions.

New conversations are needed with more stakeholders not just those entrenched and running their busy program. We can learn from China's attempt at the straddle bus, from Moller's attempt at the flying car, from Amazon's drone developments, as well as the unpublished, unknown ideas that reside in the minds of ordinary citizen stakeholders who don't currently have a seat at the table. Let's not protect a walled garden that needs to go away. The benefits awaiting us are too great.

No matter the innovation in transportation, it will mean less people are employed in the future as delivery drivers of all sorts. There are certainly social benefits to having less congestion, pollution, accidents, noise, and all of the other negative externalities that accompany transportation systems today. But, we'll need to continue to ask the question, what about the people?

We often forget about those negatively affected by progress. We certainly would be a more dystopian society if we simply eliminated the multitude of jobs associated with delivery and transportation and then shrugged our shoulders. Hmm I guess those people should have had different jobs. This reaction only adds to the dystopia.

As jobs disappear, unchecked capitalism will simply have the spoils go to whoever owns the drones or pods, or what have you. No doubt there will be new jobs, but like other waves of efficiency, the new jobs will be fewer in number like other industries that have already achieved productivity gains through automation. So, we are back to wealth and economy and social and environment. And, you are now seeing that every chapter in this book, like life is interdependent with other chapters. Few things outside the laboratory exist in complete isolation.

Next up, we'll look at the future of food and comfort. After all, now that you're no longer having to drive that driverless vehicle, perhaps you'll have a vehicular picnic, or a *vehicularnic.*

7 FOOD & COMFORT

In this chapter we'll explore comfort, but not the kind gained through transport like the last chapter. Comfort is intrinsically linked with food. If you're reading this book you've probably eaten within the last few hours. You probably ate a few hours before that, too. If you haven't eaten then you should probably put this book down and eat. You'll be more comfortable, right? Even when we're not hungry we're often preoccupied with food, like dogs dreaming of kibble or cats of self opening cans of tuna. We not only require food for nourishment and fuel, we actually find enjoyment in most things culinary.

In this chapter we're going to dream large and let our imagination run without bound.

"If more of us valued food and cheer and song above hoarded gold, it would be a merrier world."[1]

John Ronald Reuel Tolkien
English writer, poet, philologist,
academic,author
(1892–1973)

Popup Food Pill. Simply add hot water to the Popup Food Pill and presto – you've got food. Wish for any food you desire. Simply give the "steak" command while your popup food pill is generating. Remember to mention the grilled mushrooms or BBQ sauce, anything your palate desires. There is no cooking required, no preparation, no messy clean up of those pots and pans.

Sure, there has been various versions of this dream for decades. So, let's give it a refresh. Hey, if we are going to dream, let's go big.

Downloadable Food. Let's update the meal in a pill dream to instead make Downloadable Food. Imagine browsing from the visual menu on any screen: your television, computer, phone, fridge, even your eyewear. After making your selection and indicating how many servings you'd like, you give the destination and desired show time — where and when you'd like your food to appear. Press the button and voila; at the desired time the food appears on your dining room table or picnic table, or wherever is desired.

Ok so we're not quite ready for all of that fancy technology but we still have to eat, right?

That is a problem for many that go hungry even though there is an abundance of food nearby. As John Oliver revealed in a segment on Last Week Tonight with John Oliver, food waste in America alone is astonishing. Up to 40 percent of all food produced in the U.S. never gets eaten, even while nearly 50 million households across the country experience food insecurity.[2] Add to this 90 million tons of food thrown away in the European Union each year, equal to three million trucks stretched around the equator.[3]

Imagine a future where people share food much like people have opened their home and become hoteliers through services like Airbnb or put their idle cars to use through services like RelayRides.

Well, it turns out the sharing economy does include food and it is in full swing with plenty of thoughtful people and organizations participating. That is a great thing because according to projections by the World Resources Institute, by 2050 we'll need to feed 9.6 billion people.[4]

The Magnitude of Food Waste and Loss

The U.N. Food and Agriculture Organization (FAO) estimates one-third of all food produced worldwide, every year, goes to loss and waste; at a cost of about $750 billion to food producers.[5]

But, this isn't a cost only to producers; we all pay for that. And, we pay in other ways, too. Factor in the natural resources used for growing, processing, packing, transporting, and marketing and the cost of wasted and lost food increases dramatically. 28 percent of the world's agriculture land used to grow crops is wasted. That is the total land area of China, Mongolia, and Kazakhstan. Plus, the water wasted in growing that food could serve all of the household's water needs for the entire world. Imagine the forest and marine habitats that are destroyed in the quest to produce more food. The carbon footprint of food produced and not eaten is estimated to be 3.3 Gtonnes of CO_2. If these green house gases emitted were represented as a country it would be the third largest polluter, behind China and the U.S.[6]

Food produced and not eaten is a huge cost to society.

So what are social entrepreneurs doing in the food sharing economy and what is yet to be done? First, let's explore the bright spots of what is working well.

LeftoverSwap.com is a smartphone app to match those with leftover food to those who want it. Users can view leftovers near them, select and then arrange for pickup or delivery. Or, on the giving side, users can snap a picture of what they have to share and then make it available for others. The smartphone application is currently available for Google Play or the App Store. But, what about a larger scale and beyond the smartphone. Well, it turns out there is an app for that, too. Or, rather an entire platform.

FoodSharing.de is a food sharing platform that allows regular food, which would otherwise be thrown away, to be shared with people who need it.

Using the website, individuals who have food that is still good but cannot use it, connect to people who need food. But, it is more than individuals. Supermarkets and bakers are participating in over 240 German cities along with 41,000 people. In the first year of operation the website received over one million visitors.

People don't have the stigma of registering and then subsequently waiting in line at the food bank. It is more dignified. Volunteers known as foodsavers are happy to do their part in picking up food from bakers, saving food from waste, and making the world a little better place. Bakers and participating stores feel good that food that would otherwise cost them to discard is instead put to good use feeding people.

What started as one supermarket in Berlin is now over 1,980 companies in Germany, Austria, and Switzerland, where more than 9,421 foodsaver volunteers having saved over 2,200,928.5 kg of food that would have otherwise been tossed.[7] It is a win for everybody involved.

So, let's expand and improve this service. The code to make this work is already open source and free so it's really ready for expansion into other cities.

Similar efforts are underway on other continents.

RipeNear.Me in Adelaide, South Australia allows people to connect directly with growers or find food on public land. The site has the promise of eliminating waste at the source and even encourages more locally grown sustainable food in backyards, front yards, balconies, rooftops, vacant blocks, and other empty urban spaces. The platform aims to make it easy to find, share, swap, buy and sell local and homegrown foods. Growers can give away excess food or even establish a profitable ecosystem or micro farm.[8]

Solidarity Fridge. In the city of Galdakao, in the Basque town in Northern Spain, the Association of Volunteers of Galdakao, under leadership from Alvaro Saiz established the Solidarity Fridge. The communal refrigerator sits on a city sidewalk with a fence around it. Anybody in the town of 30,000 can deposit food or help themselves to what's inside. Simply stop by and grab what you need. Mayor Ibon Uribe, upon hearing the idea, immediately supported it with a small budget to get it started and to sustain its operation. A physical refrigerator in plain view is especially valuable for those without Internet access or smartphones. The group wants to build a network of communal refrigerators and invites others to join.

This isn't the only Solidarity Fridge. A similar movement in the Saudi Arabian city, Ha'il with 10 times the population, 356,876, was sparked by one man who installed a "charity fridge" outside his house. He felt that this did some good but spared the needy the shame of asking for food. Imagine other refrigerators similarly placed in public places.

Would the mayor or city manager in your city have the courage to add a Solidarity Fridge? How about leadership at your church or mosque?

I hold more confidence in citizens than politicians to make lasting change when it come to reducing food waste and loss through sharing. So, what can you do beyond more careful shopping to your specific needs? Well, like the Little Free Library movement that started with one thoughtful person in 2009 and has now exploded to over 30,000 tiny libraries around the world, you can make a difference, too. But instead of sharing a book, you can share fruits, vegetables, and the like. Plant something and then share it with your neighbors or even strangers — you know, the friends you've not yet met.

Own a restaurant or work at a supermarket? You can do even better by re-imagining dumpsters.

Community Food Box. Instead of tossing perfectly good food in the dumpster, place it in the insulated box next to the dumpster. Add an alert button. Food goes in and when you press the alert button a picture is taken of the contents and the image transmitted to the nearest services organization or food sharing apps.

Restaurants could have the same thing. But, instead of having it next to the dirty dumpster, place leftovers or food slated to be tossed, in the front or side of the restaurant. Make it ready for pickup by those without the means to dine inside.

Imagine such a Little Free Library movement, but with food instead of books. With this maybe in the future we could get to a near zero waste restaurant or grocery store.

All of these applications and services mentioned so far are free. And, so is the labor that is producing them. But for the good graces of those volunteers and their other income producing jobs or crowdfunding or donate now buttons, these sites and services are at risk of eventually rotting on the vine. This is especially true of technology platforms as they scale and require more bandwidth, server space, and human resources to deal with security, customer and community relations.

Are you seeing the problem? This is meaningful work that helps human beings and is even great for the planet. But, our economic system doesn't currently value this work, which is why these people are largely volunteers. If you were the architect of a planet's economic system, it is unlikely that you would pay employees and executives at food companies to overproduce for a profit and at great cost to society, while at the same time you would ask volunteers to make up for those shortcomings and create apps and services to redistribute the excess food. Yet we value the former and not the latter. We often place value on the wrong things.

See also: Make Meaning Department, Unconditional Universal Basic Income, and Innovation Clearinghouse

For every social entrepreneur who is trying to do some good with the food equation there are some impossible ideas just out of reach, at least for now.

All of the applications and services mentioned for food sharing are limited to vegetables, fruits, bread products, and cooked leftovers. They don't accept meat since they are unable to verify that the product has remained within safe temperature limits and it isn't too old.

Ah, but this is a solvable problem. In the food industry this is referred to as cold chain monitoring. What I envision is a low cost label that goes on food packaging that shows that the product hasn't been outside of the safe temperature range for that food, for an unsafe period of time. This tag could give stores, shoppers, and recipients of food sharing the confidence they need to still make use of the product.

While we are at it, let's expand the temperatures sensing to include spoilage.

Good or Not Tag. Imagine that when a food has started to chemically change, i.e., spoil, we detect this and change the appearance of the label so that the food can then be, sadly and properly discarded. This will eliminate food waste associated with confusing and seemingly arbitrary sell-by and use-by dates and open up more products to food sharing apps and services.

The Kitchen Chemist. For those foods that have been opened and the labels already removed, let's provide a kitchen appliance that can sample and sense a food's content, detecting any spoilage. The Kitchen Chemist alerts users to food that if consumed will pose a danger; it notices the minute changes in food spoilage microorganisms. But, The Kitchen Chemist also alerts you to foods containing your known allergens, toxic metals such as mercury, and chemical residues left behind from the use of insecticides, fungicides, herbicides, and other agricultural chemicals.

Fruit Reset. Ok, let's dream a little larger. What if our bananas are ripening too quickly or we accidentally pressed a finger a bit too hard into our avocado? That is precisely when we need Fruit Reset. Simply pass it under the faucet or refrigerator attachment and enjoy your refreshed fruit. It is as though you've walked backwards in time.

Fruit Forecast Label. This label looks at current conditions and let you know the optimal time of ripeness. Then you choose to eat that tasty morsel or give it away, refrigerate it, or reset and start over.

Food Magnet. Worried about nefarious ingredients in your food? Me too! Pass the configurable Food Magnet over your food and you'll be able to extract specified allergens such as tree nuts other nefarious items that you may not want to eat such as high fructose corn syrup, monosodium glutamate, or sodium nitrite. This is especially valuable when you are out and about and don't have access to your Kitchen Chemist.

While we are at it let's redesign that vessel that most of use to store our food, the refrigerator. First let's make it modular, repairable, upgradeable instead of fragile and disposable. See the related Fix Anything Attendant.

Instant Chill Drawers. Next, let's repurpose the mostly misunderstood crisper drawers and in their place provide Instant Chill Drawers. Like a microwave oven, but in reverse for those times when we need to cool something down. Place an item in the Instant Chill Drawer, set the temperature or condition, and remove it when ready. Now that ice-cream left on the counter is restored to its fluffy original state and the Pinot Grigio is instantly cooled.

Shelf Appear. Many times we could use a helping hand, especially when putting away groceries, laundry, or working on a project. Shelf Appear is the shelf that appears on command in just the needed size. Carrying breakfast in bed to a loved one and need to open the door? Shelf Appear will save you in this situation, too And, you thought drone technology was only for delivering packages and vacuuming hardwood floors.

The popup instant shelf sometimes needs to offer a little more dexterity, not solely a platform.

Personal Comfort Hand Hover. For those times when you have an itch in the middle of your back or there isn't anybody body around to receive you command of, "Here hold this for a second, will you?" No problem! The Personal Comfort Hand Hover can position itself in the perfect location as you go about driving, reading your book, or even delivering that sermon. In transparent mode, the Personal Comfort Hand Hover penetrates shoes or thick winter garments. There is no need to take off those warm winter mittens to get that pesky itch just out of reach.

Thoughtful automobile manufacturers in the future (of the driver or driverless variety) will add a Personal Comfort Hand Hover to vehicles in order to assist occupants with grocery bags, after shopping.

Concierge Chair. You'll never be more relaxed than in the Concierge Chair. As you sit down the height adjusts to meet you at the perfect level. But, that's not all. This chair also detects your tension points and automatically begins massaging your aches away. Have something on your mind? There is no need to talk to that search application on your smartphone or computer; the concierge chair understands your questions before you even ask them. It gently guides you toward enlightenment and comfort with each question answered. View the answers on the attached hover screen, in your eyewear, or audibly as you relax with your eyes closed.

Food Chippy. It's a sad fact. Too many of us are carrying around too much weight. Whether we are full on obese, morbidly obese, or simply a little pudgy, it isn't healthy. The weight doesn't suddenly appear. Remember the day old bread theory? Things happen gradually and then suddenly. We wake up one day and think, wow those pants are not very comfortable.

Food Chippy helps you combat this slow personal health decay. It monitors all of the food you consume. Its tiny sensing body isn't detectable to the wearer and is installed during a routine dental exam. Sitting behind a tooth, it captures data on all of what you've eaten. It can be used to help guide a more disciplined lifestyle, but it can also be used to correlate how certain foods make you feel.

Widespread use of Food Chippy has the promise of ending the diabetes pandemic and putting it in the museum for good.

Food Chippy paired with the Personal Comfort Hand Hover will protect you from yourself. In fat smacker mode, when you try to eat too much, the hand hover inflicts a little corporal punishment. It delivers a good old fashioned slap. The audible command that accompanies it is simple, "No! Stop eating." But, many Food Chippy enabled applications will be more pleasant.

Chapter Summary

Comfort really does correlate to food. Too little and you go hungry and too much you get fat. Neither of those extreme conditions are very comfortable. We do have an abundance of food especially if we all participate in growing local, curtail our poor habits around consumption, and reduce loss and waste. We can redistribute some of that food like the Dream Cream of chapter one helped us to redistribute fat. But, in this case, the Dream Cream is the collection of food sharing apps and services and we are redistributing fat while it is still in food form.

We can do many things that eliminate waste and get food redistributed so nobody goes hungry — some are more possible than others. This chapter revealed some impossipreneurs who are becoming less so, as their applications and services become the norm.

But, for many, at the end of the day (and the beginning, too) most of us would probably rather escape into our bubble, relax in our concierge chair while being massaged and entertained. Oh, yeah, let's not forget the hand hover that delivers our favorite drink, maybe even retrieved from the neighborhood Solidarity Fridge. But, what about when all of our personal bubbles collide with each other or the outside world. Maybe we should fix that. Ah, welcome to the next chapter.

8 SOCIAL

The word *social* originates from Latin *socialis*. It means companion, ally, or friend. When we think of social we may automatically think of society, but we probably don't think "friend." Modern day society doesn't exactly conjure up images of peace, harmony, and friendship. At the time of this writing the world is in the midst of the worst refugee crisis since World War II.[1] Human beings are being displaced because of war, environmental degradation, poverty, and human rights violations.

People are fleeing their own nations for safer surroundings and a restart. Some leaders and citizens welcome these human refugees whereas xenophobes treat them as enemy combatants and threats. While some lose their humanity others exercise human principles from the outset or become reacquainted with such principles as they summon them from a deeper dormant state within.

Too much of what could be a peaceful civil society with "friends" all around is instead rife with conflict. We find conflict between generations, genders, race, and potentially between any two individuals with an opposing point of view about anything. We find conflict within nations and between nations, or at least among the leaders of those nations. Many people within nations even have conflict with those that purport to lead them.

The story is much the same for the environment, more discord. If endangered species or fragile ecosystems could migrate like human refugees we'd see tracks of land and entire species move to more sanguine surroundings.

Why do we have so much conflict? Conflict occurs when something invades our personal bubble. We feel threatened either physically, emotionally, or economically. We struggle or there is disagreement, opposing points of view.

None of us are free of conflict. It has happened to me, to you, to all of us. Sometime we are the ones inflicting the harm. Worse yet, we may not realize we are doing it. This is especially true when the other party to the conflict doesn't have as strong a voice as yours. It could be a person less articulate that you or more vulnerable such as a child, a cat, a squirrel, a fish, or even a river, a tree, or patch of grass.

The absence of an opposing voice does not mean freedom from conflict and silence certainly does not mean consent. After all, you'll never hear a tree scream, "Please stop cutting me" or a river shout, "Get that crud off, stop polluting me." Most people will never be vocal to oppose the actions or inaction of powerful politicians and corporate leaders.

So, we need new ways in the world, to protect all of us, from some of us.

Might does not make right, but it is an efficient dominator and capable of promulgating propaganda. It takes a courageous person like Malala Yousafzai to oppose such momentum. Before she was even a teenager, she wrote a blog under a pseudonym for the BBC detailing her life under Taliban occupation. She advocated for girls education in her native valley where the Taliban had at times banned girls from attending school. On October 9, 2012, a Taliban assassin boarded her school bus, asked for her by name, and fired three shots at her, one of which struck her in the head.[2] She lived to continue her fight and further fuel her movement.

"I speak not for myself but for those without voice ... those who have fought for their rights ... their right to live in peace, their right to be treated with dignity, their right to equality of opportunity, their right to be educated."

Malala Yousafzai
Humanitarian, activist for female education,
former blogger for BBC Urdu under pseudonym,
co-recipient 2014 Nobel Peace Prize [3]
(Born 12 July 1997)

All reasonable people would conclude that Yousafzai is on the right side of history and that the Taliban is wrong. After all, we should be educating girls not shooting them in the face and destroying their schools. Other examples of right and wrong abound, throughout history and up to today. Take a moment away from reading this and peruse the online or print headlines around you; you'll see opposing forces across the world as well as in your own community.

The nature of conflict matters. Two neighbors that disagree on the how the cost of a fence should be apportioned between them is far different than whether or not to shut off water to residents, recruit child soldiers, deprive girls of education, force children into labor, or destroy the tents of people experiencing homelessness.

In some communities any one of these practices might be acceptable by some. Moral relativists take the view that moral judgments are true or false only relative to some particular standpoint. They believe there is no universal right and wrong.

It is understandable where this antiquated thinking comes from. The word morality originates in *mores*, meaning the customs and conventions of a community. But, where do we draw the circle for community? Do we draw it at the bounds of my property, my neighborhood, the city in which I live, the state, the country, the continent? Community isn't solely defined by people living in a particular place. It is a feeling of fellowship with other human beings that share similar values, beliefs, even aspirations.

So, in that sense, since I value education for girls, Malala and I are in the same community as are millions of other people across the globe.

On August 24, 2015, for the first time, Facebook recorded one billion logins during a single day, a milestone.[4] That is one in seven people on Earth. An even higher percentage of people given that two-thirds of the world's population are not yet connected to the Internet.[5]

If the Facebook community of users in that single day were represented as a country, they would be the third most populous country, behind China and India. I believe that they too, would side with Malala and me, that girls should be educated.

Moral relativist are wrong. There is a universal right and wrong when it comes to matters of humanity. In fact, it's spelled out in the Universal Declaration of Human Rights, adopted by the United Nations General Assembly on 10 December 1948.[6] We need to start living those values. It is time we abandon our thinking that it is okay for others to behave badly if it is within their own community. On our increasingly tiny planet, there is no such thing as their own community; we're one big community when it comes to human and environmental issues.

Thugs, goons, ignorant residents of the planet, warlords, war hawks, plutocrats, Taliban, reckless Wall Street financial engineers, exploitative executives, corrupt government officials, and others who would harm the environment, the rights of men and women, or retard social progress, take notice. The emergent global citizen is becoming less tolerant of your harmful actions. There is also no impunity for crimes against humanity and the environment. And, the statute of limitations is without expiration.

The good news is, the emergent global citizenry wants to help and it is offering you reform.

On the day he was elected leader of the Labour Party, 12 September 2015, in his first public appearance after he won the leadership vote, Jeremy Corbyn spoke in Parliament Square at the Palace of Westminster in London.

In his speech to the crowd of 100,000 concerned citizens and the world who would later listen, he said, "Our objective ought to be to find peaceful solutions to the problems of this world. Surely we have a principle between us all. We are all human beings on the same planet." He went on to say that is wasn't going to be simple. Well, it might be more simple than we think.

That brings us to our first impossible solution, the **Depolarization Unit.** This anti-extremist, anti-narcissistic, unit is part campaign and part people. It is everywhere, embedded in our lives. It forces us to be better global citizens. It isn't about a particular point of view, ideology, or religious doctrine. All of those can peacefully co-exist. However, when they don't, then we need the help of the Depolarization Unit. At first, the unit aims to expose the perpetrators to facts, not ideology, in effort to build more tolerance and acceptance. In essence, it works to change their belief filters. It works in concert with the Truth Sculpture.

When we have one view of the truth and it is still disregarded for one's own advantage at the harm of others or the environment then more help is needed.

It is hard for people to stay dry in a dunk tank. The Depolarization Unit is like that, but instead of using water it uses information, influence and conversation. The perpetrator finds themselves surrounded by empathetic global citizens who soak them in humanity and truth.

They are subjected to more productive conversations. They'll find that they are better able to connect their thoughts and their hearts to the truth, as opposed to some ideology, prejudice, or antiquated practice.

Like a parent explaining to children that they must share, or take turns, the Depolarization Unit becomes the global parent. Here is what it would sound like if you listened on. "Now [insert name here], you can't invade this territory, there are indigenous people living there. Or, [insert other name here], you must stop building that missile system, there is no humane use for it. Or, [yet another name here], respect the rights of others. Theft is not becoming of a good global citizen."

The world has a recent example of the type of person well suited for the Depolarization Unit. Icelandic actor and activist, Hörður Torfason, organizer of the Orange Army, a non violence civilian patrol meant to minimize the possibility of violence, is such a person.[7]

In 2008 when Iceland's economy collapsed, people were understandably angry. Some people wanted to incite violence. When violent protestors began throwing rocks at police, the Orange Army stepped in between, preventing further escalation, protecting police and all citizens.[8]

The Depolarization Unit can work on individuals but it can also work on organizations, too, even the government, as was the case in Iceland. Torfason invited his fellow citizens into a conversation with the aim of answering two seemingly simple questions:

1) What has happened to our country?
2) What are we going to do about it?

From those questions Torfason and his fellow citizens built an unprecedented movement in the tiny Nordic country. Dubbed the Kitchenware Revolution or Pots and Pans Revolution, the movement eventually did achieve all four of the Icelandic protesters' demands, namely:[9]

1) Resignation of the prime minister and cabinet;
2) Resignation of the Central Bank's board;
3) Resignation of the Financial Security Authority's board;
4) New elections as soon as possible

But, what if the collapse of Iceland's economy could have been prevented? There are always signs. Remember the day old bread theory - things happen gradually and then suddenly. In the case of Iceland, the failed banks were issuing loans to the principal owners of those banks and in some cases such lending was nearly equal to the bank's capital base.[10] It was reckless and unsustainable.

Wrongdoing was discovered later, but was there no human being that was aware? Of course there was. What is likely is that there was no would-be whistleblower on the tiny island with the courage to do so. After all, it is an island. There was also a prevailing attitude of suspending the belief that the good times will have to end at some point. Few people ever dare to be the proverbial wet blanket.

In other cases, whistleblowers have come forward. If you recall, Sherron Watkins, a former Enron employee, was such a whistleblower who exposed one of the largest accounting frauds in history.[11] Her testimony along with the subsequent five-year investigation led to the conviction of Enron ex-CEO, Jeff Skilling and founder, Kenneth Lay on fraud and conspiracy charges.[12][13]

Other whistleblowers have come forward in many areas

of business and government. History is the ultimate judge of whether these whistleblowers are justified. In older cases we generally accept the principled actions these people took to notify others during their own heightened moment of consciousness.

This is true of the leaking of the Pentagon Papers by Daniel Ellsberg to the New York Times.[14] The secret account of the Vietnam War revealed deception by decades of presidential administrations. Ellsberg sparked a political controversy that resulted in charges against him that carried a combined sentence of 115 years. But, all charges against Ellsberg were eventually dropped on May 11, 1973.[15] We now look back and think, of course he did the right thing. Likewise, for the toxicologist Myron Mehlman, who had just been nominated to the National Academy of Sciences by his employer, Mobil Oil Corporation. What did he do wrong? While presenting to corporate managers in Japan about the health effects of gasoline he learned that the wholly owned Japanese subsidiary of Mobil was selling gasoline containing dangerously high levels of the known carcinogen, benzene. He warned that the levels should be reduced or advised they stop selling it. Upon his return to the United States he was fired. Mehlman filed suit against Mobil and eventually won $3.5 million in punitive damages.[16]

The list of whistleblowers is long and the subjects being reported nearly just as long involving: sex trafficking, improper labeling of food and medicine, banking and accounting fraud, improper handling of nuclear waste, drug trafficking, price fixing, environmental degradation, presidential politics, espionage, even tweaking cigarettes to make them even more addictive. More recently add to the list torture, killing of civilians, illegal arms trafficking, tax evasion using Swiss bank accounts and also accounts in the Cayman Islands, systematic racial profiling, healthcare fraud, robo-signing, adulterated pharmaceuticals, and the illegal surveillance of innocent citizens.

In nearly every case, the whistleblower is initially made out to be the enemy. It's as though the worse crime is to upset the steady state of affairs no matter how unwholesome or gruesome they may be. This is especially evident for federal whistleblowers.

In the U.S., whistleblower protection laws have really provided little to no protection at all because the court with the exclusive jurisdiction, the Unites State Court of Appeals for the Federal Circuit, has narrowly defined the types of disclosure that qualify for whistleblower protection.[17] It is likely that most waste, fraud, and abuses that people wish to report fall outside of the definition and remain unreported for fear of joining the ranks of the unprotected, persecuted, and prosecuted. Sadly, the situation isn't any different in other governments and intergovernmental organizations. The Special Rapporteur for Freedom of Expression at the United Nations released a report on October 14, 2015 with recommendations for protecting whistleblowers.[18]

History will be the ultimately judge as we look back 100 years from now and decide what was morally reprehensible. I'd suggest that the actions of the soldiers in the U.S. Apache helicopter opening fire on a group of civilians in Eastern Baghdad (footage leaked to WikiLeaks from U.S. Pvt. Bradley Manning that currently has over 15 million view on YouTube[19][20]) are every bit as morally reprehensible as a Taliban assassin shooting Malala in the face. Today, we can easily look back on the practice of human slavery or child labor and view them as morally reprehensible. Perhaps whistleblowers are better than others at projecting themselves into the future and making such judgments about the present. They only wish history and humanity would catch up to them.

"When a soldier who shared information with the press and public is punished far more harshly than others who tortured prisoners and killed civilians, something is seriously wrong with our justice system," said Ben Wizner, director of the American Civil Liberties Union's Speech, Privacy and Technology Project. "This is a sad day for Bradley Manning, but it's also a sad day for all Americans who depend on brave whistleblowers and a free press for a fully informed public debate."

Imagine a society free of the need to even have whistleblowers. Until we reach that point in our own human evolution we'll need to continue to put bad actions and the people behind them in the spotlight. We'll also need to protect whistleblowers from personal harm, economic ruin, and imprisonment that so many of them face.[21]

"Citizens with a conscience are not going to ignore wrong-doing simply because they'll be destroyed for it: the conscience forbids it."

Edward Joseph Snowden
American privacy activist, technologist,
former CIA officer, NSA contractor
whistleblower currently in exile
(born June 21, 1983)

In 2013, while working as an NSA contractor, Edward Snowden discovered classified evidence the U.S. government was, contrary to its public statements, secretly operating a global system of mass surveillance that extended far beyond the search for terrorists. The eavesdropping on U.S. citizens and foreign leaders was in violation of human rights standards and international law. Snowden joined the long list of whistleblower when he leaked information to journalists, whose stories then appeared in international newspapers.[22][23] The U.S. Department of Justice has since sought Edward Snowden to answer their charges. Russia meanwhile has granted Snowden asylum where he is in exile today.

As with many whistleblowers, some view them as heroes while other wish to see them blacklisted, bankrupted, and broken. Though U.S. authorities are on one side of history, other organizations have taken a different stance. Snowden has been awarded with the Sam Adams Award for Integrity in Intelligence, the Stuttgart Peace Prize 2014, and the Right Livelihood Award, the latter of which rewards outstanding vision and work on behalf of our planet and its people. Bestowing the award on Snowden, they shared, "for his courage and skill in revealing the unprecedented extent of state surveillance violating basic democratic processes and constitutional rights." Snowden has received many other awards and recognition. Again, history will ultimately catch up to a more just future.

Whistleblower Insurance Fund. Providing a safety net to whistleblowers is like providing a life vest to whitewater rafters. But instead of surviving torrents of water it empower people with courage and provides them safe passage so they can inform the public that bad things are happening.

This safety net is for people to sound the alarm when they see a culture gone awry, whether it is involved in financial engineering, food production, emission scandals, government abuse, healthcare fraud, military wrongdoing, or some other area of society.

If a whistleblower advances an accusation and then subsequently gets fired as a result of it, instead of having to crowdfund their way back to financial health they can draw against the safety net aka Whistleblower Insurance Fund.

The safety net is funded through fees paid by the perpetrators of past egregious behaviors. In that sense, it is an insurance policy organizations and even governments pay into, triggered by their past bad behavior. It could be corrective in that people will feel safer to sound the alarm earlier, thereby possible preventing forthcoming disastrous and more costly circumstances. So, who would fund such an insurance scheme if it existed today? For starters, the banks and financial institutions that engaged in financial engineering that brought about the global financial crisis, automotive makers who delayed recalls that knowingly killed unwitting vehicle occupants, oil companies that have ruined ecosystems, food corporations that have sickened and killed people, tobacco companies, defense contractors, etc.

And, when a company's CEO is involved in a scandal any golden parachute they may be counting on as they resign or are fired is stripped away and repurposed for the fund. Society reclaims it. Likewise for former politicians imprisoned or forced out of office for misconduct. They forfeit their lifelong pensions and all or a portion of those funds become available to the Whistleblower Insurance Fund. When the profits are taken out of scandal and would-be whistleblowers' lives are no longer financially ruined, it may in fact stop the cycle of bad behavior. There are other precautions we can take as well.

It would be best if we correct behavior along the way, before things become so out of control that somebody needs to blow the proverbial whistle.

Norm Flags. Norms are the informal understandings that govern individual behavior in society. They are pretty unremarkable actually; they tend to be common sense and well understood. Within certain groups, especially professions, there may be certain additional norms that need to be learned. In automotive racing there is a norm of using flags to indicate track conditions and send messages to drivers. A green flag indicates the start of a race and the checkered flag, the finish. Most people know of those flags. But, there are other flags reserved for caution, unsportsmanlike conduct, disqualification and to declare a temporary stop to the race.

We need flags in our organizations to similarly indicate the current conditions and performance and also to send messages as visible as waving flags.

A person needs to be able to send a message not only to leadership but to every person in the organization that there is the equivalent of "dangerous debris on the track" or "someone has engaged in unwholesome activity." It is key that the Norm Flags are visible by everybody, not solely leadership. This creates an atmosphere of mutual accountability that absolves nobody in the organization of wrongdoing in the event of a major downfall. In the case of Enron's fall from fame, if such a system were in place, then the arrogance and intimidation that came from the top would have been dampened by the collective power of individuals.

System Reset. When there are persistent or frequent flags in an organization or operation that has stakeholders concerned then any one of those individual stakeholders should be able to declare a system breakdown and perform a System Reset.

Much like your sluggishly performing computer or phone may require a periodic reset, organizations need to be tuned periodically, too. Maybe business conditions have changed and it no longer makes sense to stay on the same path. Imagine you were an 18th century captain of a merchant ship under contract with the British government to transport criminals to the new world. But, the pesky little American Revolution had the victors in a position to refuse acceptance of any further criminals. If that were you, you'd wish you had reset your system before you sailed prisoners across an ocean and back returning home to demand payment, but unable to do so, still holding your unwanted human cargo.

The System Reset is reserved for those situations when things no longer feel right. Any whistleblower eventually gets to that point, but the key is to sound the alarms, wave the flags, and declare a System Reset before the Great Depression, before the human atrocities, environmental degradation, civil war, sexual abuse of children, refugee crisis, etc.

Recently, two phenomenal things have occurred. First, the former owner of the now defunct Peanut Corporation of America was sentenced to 28 years in prison for his role in a salmonella outbreak that killed 9 people and sickened hundreds. And secondly, the CEO of Volkswagen resigned amid the discovery of emission cheating vehicle software and the subsequent battering of the company's stock.

Where was the human voice in all of this? Where was the voice of reason and compassion that said, "Whoa, hold on we need to slow down here. This doesn't seem right."

In each of these cases had there been Norm Flags and a System Reset, the imprisoned owner would instead be enjoying this weekend with his family and the Volkswagen stock would not have shed one third of its value. The price of following the wrong path can be extremely high. Ask any former Enron employee. Inaction can be just as costly.

Though each of these events are very different from one another they do share a common characteristic. They exhibit a culture of not caring. Somebody within those companies should have been able to declare a System Reset. That is, unless it was a homogeneous culture comprised of similarly uncaring people. I don't think that was the case. I think there are some good people within most organizations, including these two but, they either didn't have the courage or didn't know where or how to sound the alarm. As Sherron Watkins of the defunct Enron has shared, good people became frustrated and left or they reacted by posting messages in online message boards.

This sentiment is echoed by Beatrice Edwards, the

former international director of Government Accountability Project, a nonprofit public interest group that promotes government and corporate accountability by defending whistleblowers. In working with U.N. Whistleblowers, she shared, "Many would-be whistleblowers resign rather than endure the protracted and complex internal process."[24] Her book, *The Rise of the American Corporate Security State: Six Reasons to Be Afraid*, tells much from her perspective of working with whistleblowers who witnessed wrongdoing firsthand.

Let's give people Norm Flags and the ability to declare the System Reset so that we can keep the future unbroken as it unfolds.

Imagine these abilities coupled with a culture of care as Pope Francis shared in his address to members of the U.S. Congress:

"In Laudato Si', I call for a courageous and responsible effort to 'redirect our steps', and to avert the most serious effects of the environmental deterioration caused by human activity. I am convinced that we can make a difference and I have no doubt that the United States – and this Congress – have an important role to play. Now is the time for courageous actions and strategies, aimed at implementing a 'culture of care' and 'an integrated approach to combating poverty, restoring dignity to the excluded, and at the same time protecting nature'. We have the freedom needed to limit and direct technology; to devise intelligent ways of directing, developing and limiting our power; and to put technology 'at the service of another type of progress, one which is healthier, more human, more social, more integral.' In this regard, I am confident that America's outstanding academic and research institutions can make a vital contribution in the years ahead."[25]

Yes, humanity and the environment would benefit from a culture of care. We should all walk together on a path of advancing human progress while having a more civil society and sustainable environment. Pope Francis is but one messenger among many that espouse a people first agenda. At 1.2 billion followers, he's noteworthy to mention. You can be noteworthy, too. Advance a culture of care beginning in your home, at school, in your community, at work, and in the online community.

Hopefully, Pope Francis moved Congress to focus forward, to a new era, a "people first" era that confronts reality, embraces science, respects natural resources, and advances prosperity for all households, even the people who don't currently have one.

We need to reduce the conflict across the spectrum of human civilization. This includes conflict against each other and conflict with the environment. Even though you might not literally have Norm Flags (yet) and a System Reset in your home, at work, and in your other social circles, it doesn't make you any less powerful in enacting them. If you have the courage then you can declare a yellow flag. You can go even further and use the black flag to disqualify someone, even an organization, for unsportsmanlike conduct. You can declare a System Reset. If and when we do this, we will be acting like good global citizens.

Humanity Dashboard. When I was young my brother and I walked to the corner grocery store up the street from my Grandparent's home. We had exchanged some bottles for cash and with the proceeds bought some snacks. Shortly after leaving the store, my brother opened his store-bought sandwich and casually tossed the packaging to the ground.

A man in a parked car nearby shouted out his window, "Hey, pick up that garbage." My brother did, without hesitation. In this case, a good global citizen checked my brother's littering behavior. I think it had a long standing effect. Years later it was my brother who initiated cleanup at the Climber's Bivouac Trailhead where we camped while waiting to gain permits to climb Mt. Saint Helens, in Washington State. The dumpsters were overflowing with trash and people futilely piled garbage on top even though it immediately spilled to the ground. It was as though instead of throwing it directly on the ground, they felt the need to "tag" the top of the heap first, as though that was the proper thing to do. We grew tired of watching this.

A few of us joined my brother in compacting what trash was in the dumpster, making room for more. We even set aside bags we filled with obvious recyclables though there was not yet such a feature at the campground. We'd have initiated a Norm Flag if we could have.

With bags of recyclables and room in the dumpster people started behaving differently.

Imagine if we all had lenses through which we could view our decisions or those of our employer, our church, our government, etc. We could answer the question about how a particular stakeholder would view a particular decision or action. Think of this as a more humane version of the spreadsheet. Instead of calculating numbers we could view decisions through a stakeholder lens. And, those stakeholders could be a wide assortment including: member, customer, donor, investor, visitor, prisoner, voter, citizen, tenant, resident, student, guest, traveler, passenger, performer, elected officials, inspector, shopper, licensee, owner, parishioner, supplier, vendor, consultant, partner, board member, adviser, council member, leader, refugee, patron, staff, volunteer, client, shareholder, agency, patient, child, doctor, administrator, buyer, licensee, immigrant, soldier, driver, guide, occupant, person experiencing homelessness, employee, taxpayer.

Not all stakeholders are apparent at first thought. Consider audiences who may not be vocal or visible including: people with disabilities, pets and domesticated animals, animals in nature, environmental resources, etc.

The Humanity Dashboard would be an application

much like we use spreadsheets today. But, whereas spreadsheets fall short, forcing us into abstract views and potentially callous decisions, the Humanity Dashboard would make stakeholders come alive. We could see the faces and images of those who are impacted by decisions and actions or even our inactions. We get to see things from their perspective and get a better sense of what they think and feel. This would be good for all stakeholders involved. This is a good method to test our behavior against an audience who may not be like ourselves. I created an actual test for employees to use in a software company that I previously started. I called it the reasonable investor test.

Reasonable Investor Test. In 1998, I started a software company. As the founding CEO, it didn't take very long to realize I had at least two full-time jobs, namely raising capital and building the organization's operations. Eventually we hired an outside CEO to help. I took the reigns as the Chief Operating Officer. As the company grew I couldn't, nor did I want to, be party to every decision or attend every meeting. This didn't keep employees from continuing to seek my approval. I devised a test they could employ on their own without me in the room. I called it the reasonable investor test.

I explained it to them like this. When you are trying to decide or take a certain course of action, imagine yourself presenting to a panel of sixteen reasonable investors. Imagine they've politely assembled, seated across from you at a large table, and are looking you directly in the eye. You are about to explain to them the decision you plan to make or the action you intend to take. If you can look them in the eye and justify the decision or expenditure, then it passes the test. If you have some reservations and would not be willing to do this, then you should probably reconsider your decision or action.

I concocted this test after our CEO and VP of Sales

decided to prematurely celebrate a customer win by indulging in a lavish and expensive meal for themselves. I begrudgingly approved the expense, but I didn't think reasonable investors would have appreciated their invested money being spent this way. We never did win that customer and the CEO and VP of Sales never understood or embraced the Reasonable Investor Test. But, I think other employees did and I've also shared the story with other entrepreneurs and now you.

Life should be ruled by more than the spreadsheet or the whim of who's in charge.

A culture of care, like life, is a bit more complicated than what might initially appear favorable on a spreadsheet or what one might feel like doing at the moment. I'm guessing the former CEO of the Peanut Corporation of America might today consider more stakeholders. I'm also guessing that the former CEO of Volkswagen might employ some sort of reasonable stakeholder test for employees to use in guiding their own work or that of colleagues. Investors are not the only stakeholders just like spreadsheets are not the only tool. There are many other stakeholders to be considered not the least of which are customers, employees, and the environment. Closer to home, stakeholders might include neighbors, the community and even members of your household.

Brain Retrain. It doesn't matter where your beliefs fall in the age old nature versus nurture debate. You must admit that people are shaped in part by what they learn and hear over and over again. As with all propaganda repetition is key.

You hear something often enough and you will begin to believe it. And, if the subject provokes negative emotions, chances are your slow-to-evolve brain will especially remember it. For the most part, this feature has been good for you and your ancestors. Memories of what you know to be dangerous or threatening are stored like indelible ink in your brain. It is why you're likely to seek safety if you see a tiger walking toward you on the sidewalk.

But, our evolutionary faculties allow us to be led astray as well. Just as a computer can be programmed to run a set of instructions, you can be programmed through propaganda to believe things that are not actually based in fact. Make the lies more emotional and they become more memorable, if not outright believable. Political strategist employ this technique through the use of polarizing negative ads for precisely this reason. Some countries and the European Union exert various levels of regulation on ad content and delivery mechanisms, but in the United States, it is largely unrestricted and laissez-faire.

If you are in the U.S. it is likely you can easily recall a negative attack ad from previous elections. But, can you recall any happy, positively focused ads that actually highlight a candidate's qualifications or what they hope to achieve? Yeah, me neither.

This is problematic because ideology and lies to back it up, can reign supreme over a fact based reality. History shows that in the extreme, people can be marginalized, even made out to be less than human, mere bugs that few have remorse in squashing. Visit any Holocaust memorial and you'll see the symptoms of such. Try to read the names you see inscribed, aloud. You won't be able to, even if you try. First it would take too long. But, more importantly, it turns out half of the names would not appear. You cannot read a page that does not exist, not in this book and not in history.

It turns out, there is another half of the Holocaust that has gone unreported.

Most people are aware of Nazi death camps where Nazis systematically murdered millions of people, the most infamous being Auschwitz located in Poland. There were numerous others, too. But, what most people don't realize is that at least a couple of million more human beings were executed without ever boarding a death train or seeing the inside of a camp. No, these humans were executed in the villages they called home. You see, after the Germans invaded the Soviet Union in 1941 they systematically gathered, shot, and killed Jews, Roma, and other victims locally in Eastern Europe and the former Soviet Union. Mobile death squads killed in place.

Because the cold war following World War II kept the physical locations and records off limits, much of this story is only just now unfolding thanks to Father Patrick Desbois and the work of the organization he founded in 2004, Yahad – In Unum. The name of the organization is a combination of words, Yahad, a Hebrew word meaning "together" with the Latin phrase In Unum, meaning "in one."

The organization is corroborating physical evidence with soviet records and interviews along with surviving witness testimony from the villages where the executions occurred. They refer to this largely unknown and untold story as the "Holocaust by Bullets."[26]

As Father Desbois points out, "Genocide is a human disease that sleeps and awakens from one generation to the next." In a 60 Minutes interview of Father Desbois, correspondent Lara Logan asked, "Why does it matter, all these years later?"

"It matters because it still happens," he tells her. "It's not the past, unfortunately. It seems to be part of the future. Like the Nazis, ISIS fighters feel justified in killing those who are different," Desbois explains.[27]

Yahad – In Unum recognizes that the massacres in Cambodia, Rwanda, Darfur, the Balkans and Syria have all been modeled after the same systematic tactics carried out during the "Holocaust by Bullets."[28]

Part of the work of Yahad – In Unum is to surface the truth about the mass executions that happened outside of Nazi concentration camps. They provide evidence of mass executions to answer the Holocaust deniers of today and tomorrow. They also spread awareness and help educate people about the lessons to be learned about genocide. In the evidence gathering and storytelling it is extremely important they include video testimonials with the aging witnesses from the villages, now in their eighties and nineties.[29]

We all share the same humanity so it is important that we understand the horrific history and educate present and future generations to prevent what Father Desbois refers to as the global epidemic of modern genocide.

It is easy for the modern military-industrial-political complex to propagandize and justify its role in and around these genocides. Personnel working in the international association Médecins Sans Frontières (MSF), or Doctors Without Borders, are largely volunteers providing assistance to populations in distress, to victims of natural or man-made disasters, and to victims of armed conflict. They do so irrespective of race, religion, creed, or political convictions.

The war machine and the people who power it, by contrast, have the motivation of profit from the onset and will manufacture conflict to justify its continued existence.

If war was not profitable for those involved it would have already been put in the museum. Those industries and people would be doing something else.

Instead, politicians and wannabes dependent upon campaign contributions from the military-industrial complex represent those industries and their interests.

When the politician gets elected their loyalty and the truth they represent flows accordingly thereafter.

**"Political language — and with variations
this is true of all political parties, from
Conservatives to Anarchists — is designed
to make lies sound truthful
and murder respectable,
and to give an appearance of solidity
to pure wind."**[30]

Eric Arthur Blair
pen name George Orwell
novelist, essayist, journalist, critic
(1903–1950)

Because of these modern day realities, retraining our
brains is critical. We see things as truths that are anything
but — things such as if you are poor it's your own fault or
as an American you are in serious danger of being killed by
a terrorist.

Another favorite lie that gets passed along as truth is a
tenet of neoliberalism that has persisted for decades, since it
first permeated the economic policies of Margaret Thatcher
in the United Kingdom and Ronald Reagan in the United
States. It is the notion that if you cut taxes on the wealthy
then prosperity will trickle down to the middle class and lift
the poor out of poverty. This is absurd and not based in any
reality. People who still believe this do so out of sheer
ignorance or are bridled by ideology that was cooked up at a
point in time.

With the trickle-down economic theory, the cooker was
Milton Friedman and the origin was 1970. If it was ever
true, which I think it was not, it certainly didn't bear out
over time. I suspect that if Freidman were alive today and
he were genuinely truthful, he'd have to reassess his own
theory. Nearly 50 million Americans are experiencing
poverty according to recent U.S. Census Bureau data. If this
is a people problem, then these problems lay squarely with
the policy makers and corporate executives whose actions

continue to gut the middle class, not with that middle class whose lives have been negatively affected.

Mainstream media is complicit in the spread of propaganda, too. Giving them a little credit, many of them may simply be ignorant themselves. After all, American and European media have scored low on the "How not to be ignorant about the world" test created by Hans and Ola Rosling of the Gapminder Foundation.[31] Without any bad intention media may be using outdated facts and personal bias, shaping a world view that doesn't measure up to reality.

The media can also be unwitting puppets freely covering the propagandistic work of multinational corporations and governments dutifully regurgitating the requisite talking points. John Stewart famously and routinely made fun of the media outlets and pundits that echoed the same talking points from a unified agenda.

But, at their worst, mainstream media intentionally projects a version of the truth that favors their own corporate interests and feeds their own profits. The consolidation of the industry hasn't helped in this regard. It also doesn't help that the fairness doctrine, which the U.S. Federal Communicational Commission (FCC) used to govern broadcast communications since 1949, fizzled away. Prior to that, in exchange for a broadcast license, an operator agreed to present controversial issues of public importance and to do so in a manner that was in the Commission's view – honest, equitable, and balanced. They had to cover both or multiple sides of issues and not appear wholly biased. They also fact checked so the news reported was more rooted in reality and good intention. With the Fairness Doctrine null and void from FCC rules, the new norm has been sensationalism and entertainment in the quest for ratings and profits. The truth is, truth doesn't really matter much anymore. Facts don't mean anything more to news today than natural does to food. Huh, what?

Paying attention now? Yes, that is correct. Natural does not have a legal definition within food labeling.[32] It means bupkis, nada, nothing. Interpret it as you wish. With more people paying attention to what's in their food, especially big corporate produced food, look for more lawsuits, initiatives, and creative labeling and workarounds in this area.

Here is an example to bring together much of what I've shared. In my state of Washington, in recent years, voters through an initiative process (law by the people) voted on issues of gay marriage, legalizing recreational use of marijuana, privatizing state owned liquor stores, and mandatory labeling of foods containing genetically modified organisms (GMOs). The first three passed by a wide margin with huge voter turnout.

The GMO ballot measure failed and had lower voter turnout. You might think it curious as I did, that the one thing that affects every living creature, food, didn't get much attention. But, the other items that are voluntary in ones participation received much attention. After all, you don't have to get married at all. And, you don't have to smoke pot or drink, either. Those are all choices, not biological necessities of life. But, none of us will progress very far in life without eating. Even babies and those who can't vote are affected by what is in our food.

So, what happened? Why didn't people demonstrate they cared? Well, the pro-GMO lobby, basically the companies that profit from GMOs and putting chemicals in foods, created a hugely negative campaign that confused people, distorted facts, and of course with this they outspent the opposition by a huge margin. The truth lost and so did people that day and every day thereafter.

The time for the assault on facts is over. I could go on with even more examples, but I'm sure you see the point.

Each of us can nullify hate and ignorance by embracing and sharing facts over fiction. We can spread love not loathing. And, though each of us is not a member of the clergy like Father Desbois is, each of us can evangelize acceptance for people not like us as opposed to contributing to further dissention.

Remember we are all one. You are like me, and us like them. Remember this when you see a person experiencing homelessness. They and you are much more alike than you are different.

So when people and groups wish to rewrite history to fit a narrative that doesn't resemble the facts, there is cause for concern, especially if the lies and distortion accompany an agenda intent on doing harm.

Humans have much to learn from nature in this regard. In the animal kingdom, unless you are directly up or down the food chain from another animal, there is peaceful coexistence among animals. Most human beings don't have any interest in eating other humans – we are not in one another's food chain. We have demonstrated that as a species we can dominate, enslave, and destroy any animal on the planet including ourselves. But, what is the point in that? Let's be at least as civilized as the animals around us and peacefully co-exist. Imagine the possibilities if we repurpose our angst and tension and invest it instead into our collective humanity and our shared progress.

Rewiring our Brains for Good

Each of us can do our part to retrain the brains of all of us. Recall the earlier chapter with the Epigenetics Primer where we explored how genes get expressed through mind, mouth and muscle. Thoughts matter. Neuroscience no longer believes that the brain is fixed. Our thoughts can switch our genes on and off, altering our brain anatomy.

As Dr. Rick Hansen, author of *Hardwiring Happiness,* explains, "Your attention is like a combination spotlight and vacuum cleaner: It highlights what it lands on and then sucks it into your brain — for better or worse."

This tips the nurture versus nature debate squarely towards nurture. The brain is malleable; it isn't a static organ as was thought from the time of Descartes until a short while ago.

The relatively new study of neuroplasticity reveals that the brain can be reorganized or rewire itself due to changes in behavior, environment, neural processes, thinking, emotions, and even injury.[33] Numerous accounts of brain rewiring and healing have been demonstrated for major conditions such as stroke, learning disorders, traumatic brain injury, etc. But, our brains can also be rewired from the intruding forces of others, whether those forces are good or bad. Adolf Hitler was a heinous mad man with evil intentions. Hörður Torfason, the song-writer and activist that also became the spokesman for the organization Raddir Fólksins (Voices of the People) in 2008 following the Icelandic financial crisis, had purely good intentions.

Both men succeeded in activating the hearts and minds of others and mobilizing people to take action.

Each of them were able to put into words the feelings of so many people whom had suffered in various ways. Both offered a hopeful vision for a national (and hence personal) recovery and played to people's fears, anxieties, outrage about injustice, and even prejudices. Both of their movements gathered enough momentum to become self reinforcing without the further direct involvement of either man.

But, the similarity stops there. Hitler was a monster with demonic-like genius he used to gain power and control to do harm. By contrast, Torfason is human-centric, and though he provided the initial structure and meaning for the meetings in front of Parliament square, he gave away any potential power to the people of Iceland who sparked a new national dialogue. Some of the people who later became Members of Parliament or were elected to the Constitutional Assembly debuted at the meetings that Hörður organized.[34]

Though the messages from each man couldn't be more different, the underlying neural activities that programmed people to think and act different couldn't be more similar.

History shows that rewiring our brains can have us all supporting an evil regime that would do harm to other people if we are not careful. But, this same phenomena is also what will empower current and future generations across the planet to divorce ourselves of fossil fuels, environmental degradation, unbridled capitalism and instead program us to embrace renewable energy, shared prosperity, and to find peaceful solutions to the problems of our common world.

Like the Orange Army in Iceland, global citizens respect other people, even those not exactly like them. They also have an insatiable appetite for the truth. Don't get me wrong — life doesn't have to be all seriousness devoid of play, entertainment, and recreation. But, let's all be more discerning especially on matters of shared public interest.

Let's not embrace something that is bad for people and the planet merely because it's traditional, corporate owned media promotes it, a politician or pundit embraces it, a corporation's unquenchable thirst for growth demands it, or there is a massive public relations or advertising campaign actively working to shift our perspective.

Smoking cigarettes isn't healthy or glamorous no matter who says it, where they say it, how often they say it, or what medium they use to say it through. If you are addicted to nicotine, I'm sorry for you. I sincerely hope you'll be able to free yourself of its trappings.

Imagine instead of the U.S. Global War on Terror that has only created more hardship and conflict for the people of the world, that we instead declare a global war on intolerance, injustice, financial exclusion, marginalization of people, and the assault on truth.

Each of us has the potential to be a more powerful spokesperson and public informant than anyone of the past. Who needs mainstream media when you have social media and the Internet. If ISIS can upload public executions to proselytize their hate then a good global citizen like you can double down on good. Other global citizens like you that are concerned for people and planet will listen and amplify your message, just as I have done for the work of Father Desbois and others I've mentioned in this book and across social media.

Let's do this. Humanity has much to gain and nothing to lose, save for a little time.

Propaganda for Good. Imagine an interconnected network where each hub behaved like a good global citizen in a collective effort of Propaganda for Good. It turns out there is a precedent for such an organization. Propaganda existed in spirit long before the word itself ever did. People have always wanted to influence the hearts and minds of others and move them to action. The related word propagate is from the Latin verb *propagare*, meaning to multiply or breed. But the word propaganda actually came later in 1622, when Pope Gregory XV set up the College of Propaganda. The purpose of the college was to train missionaries who would spread Catholicism in non-Catholic countries. It was renamed in 1982 by Pope John Paul II due to the largely negative connotation surrounding the word propaganda that followed from the infamous works of Joseph Goebbels, the Minister of Propaganda in Nazi Germany.

Incidentally, the founder and father of public relations, Edward Bernays, revealed, "Modern propaganda is a consistent, enduring effort to create or shape events to influence the relations of the public to an enterprise, idea or group." He is credited with getting women to smoke cigarettes through his early work using propagandistic methods he honed after World War I and shared in his 1928 book, *Propaganda*.

His tactics can be used for good or for bad, but either way they will be effective. Hopefully, I've convinced you of the power of retraining our thinking caps and also encouraged you to be one of the forces of good. With your help we can steer the developed world in a more wholesome humane direction.

So, what will all of the companies do that are profiting handsomely off of doing bad when citizen journalism and the Propaganda for Good Network renders them less powerful, like what has happened to the tobacco companies, for example.

Good question. We'll have to return to investing in progress. We've done this before. It isn't new to us. The funny thing about progress is that it doesn't happen on its own. We have to invest in it. Progress is stubborn like that.

Invest in Progress. Imagine for a moment how big and far reaching the oil industry is. It's vast. Now imagine yourself on the day before it ever started. You are looking forward, projecting into the modern day. It is hardly imaginable. There is simply too much to consider.

The oil industry includes exploration to find reserves, extracting crude once you find it, transporting, processing, refining, redistribution, and I'm certain, a whole lot more. Its daunting. Well, most things are like that. You can do the same thought exercise with flight. Go back to the day before man ever successfully flew and then look forward. As I write this, hundreds of thousands of people on multiple continents in multiple companies are manufacturing airliners or components thereof, that will carry people to places near and far. Aside from the manufacturer and its attendant supply chain, the airline industry also comprises multiple transportation carriers whose chief concern is moving people and cargo.

Progress made in these industries and others is too far reaching and too deep to fully comprehend, even for an industry insider. You may as well try to count all of the ants, which far outnumber humans by the way.

Progress is like this. You start out with a problem you'd like to solve or an opportunity you'd like to explore. You make a little headway. Then more people get involved and build on earlier efforts. It happens in every industry including medicine, construction, law enforcement, software, retail, hospitality, food, computing, even government, etc.

As time progresses people reframe old challenges, offer up new perspectives, introduce complimentary technology, creativity, or more plainly, they apply human and financial resources. Pretty soon, an entire industry exists that outgrows every individual human contributor and organization that comprises it.

Sometimes progress needs a little kick start, a nudge. On May 25, 1961, President John F. Kennedy provided a nudge. In an address to the U.S. Congress he challenged us as a nation to safely land men on the moon by the end of the decade and safely return them home. He asked for a large commitment of resources, the largest ever by a nation during peacetime ($25 billion).[35]

On July 20, 1969, almost six years after JFK's death, Project Apollo's goal was finally realized when men landed on the moon.

At the time of Kennedy's speech, only one American had flown in space — less than a month earlier — and NASA had not yet sent a man into orbit. Even some NASA employees doubted whether Kennedy's ambitious goal could be met.[36]

Answering President Kennedy's challenge and landing men on the moon by the end of 1969 required the most sudden burst of technological creativity and the largest commitment of resources ever made by any nation in peacetime. At its peak, the Apollo program employed 400,000 people and required the support of over 20,000 industrial firms and universities.[37]

I use the "Man on the Moon" example and the subsequent Apollo program because of its historical significance and its continued impact on science and engineering. It also epitomizes "thinking big." Kennedy backed up his visionary speech with well placed bets and then marshaled the resources of an entire nation. It is interesting to think about the fact that this was all accomplished in an early state of computing and communications. This was before Google, before Microsoft, and before the Tesla of this epoch.

Think of the possibilities when you combine big thinking along with the state of technology and knowledge across science, medicine, communications, computing, industrial biotechnology, etc.

Perhaps a well coordinated open innovation initiative that marshaled the resources of multiple nations could cure cancer, solve the climate crisis, and other vexing problems that plague modern day society. Imagine Russians, Indians, Iranians, and Americans working together. Or imagine other unlikely combinations. It is possible.

The Make Meaning Departments and the Innovation Clearinghouse of Chapter 5 would leave no idle talent on the sidelines. Together, they would implore idle capital to fully participate. Like Doctors Without Borders, the work to be done is in the interest of humanity, not for a particular race, creed, religion, or political conviction.

Imagine companies that were previously on a less than wholesome track, say tobacco or oil companies, could be active participants in their own reinvention, their repositioning for good, instead of fighting tooth and claw, hanging on to their dying industries. Sadly, many corporate leaders fail to learn this lesson from the long list of failed companies that preceded them. A good exploration on that subject is Clayton Christensen book, *The Innovators Dilemma.*

Also, the human foible of thinking our own circumstances to be so unique we can't possible learn from others is explained in Daniel Gilbert's book, *Stumbling on Happiness.*

But, I'm confident in the Propaganda for Good Network and it global citizen missionaries. I think we can reframe, reform, and reshape rather than re-fail.

Summary
To quote one of early cigarette slogans that encouraged women to light up, "You've come a long way baby." That slogan worked. It was tested on women in San Francisco and was so successful it became a national campaign for Virginia Slims. Women lit up and many still do.

Our social environment is like that. We have certain people trying to get others to do something while other interests might try to prevent or stop those very actions.

Some things are very clearly right or wrong. All reasonable people would agree that the actions of the Taliban, ISIS, and Hitler described in this chapter are abhorrent.

But some items are murky and we need the help of history before we have perspective.

Our position on a subject or stance on the actions of a whistleblower might be seduced. This could be because of our loyalty to a person, allegiance to a nation, or our dependence upon an industry for our livelihood.

If we make our money in the oil industry or financial services and we have no job or income without it, then our day to day actions will likely reflect an ideology that is about protecting oil or the status quo in financial services.

This is why it is important that we have alternatives for people as well as industries. It is also why we must not declare war on them, but rather include them as we invest in progress.

When we implement new dashboards that broaden our perspective and provide safeguards for the good stewards of humanity and the environment we protect all of us, from some of us.

With those protections, especially in a highly connected network of global citizens, it is doubtful that another Hitler will rise. It is also doubtful that a Peanut Corporation of America will sicken and kill innocent consumers of its products or that VW will rig its software to cheat emissions or Enron will cook the books. More people watching is a good thing provided we know they are watching and we have an understanding. I think Edward Snowden would agree.

You have come a long way baby. Now that we've begun to understand and repair ourselves and rewire our brains for good, it's time we make some progress.

Kennedy sparked a nation to action. But we need many sparks and many nations working together. Our network for good can carry this mission. We are not starting from a dead stop. There are plenty of organizations and individuals that have already began the journey. Some of them ahead of us, some behind. No matter, it's not a race as much as its a restorative journey.

Much of the progress we need is to reshape our consumption and production patterns and rethink how we interact with our environment. In the next chapter, we'll start there, the environment.

9 ENVIRONMENT

If we're going to explore a chapter by the name of environment we should first arrive at a mutual understanding of what exactly do we mean by environment.

So, I've been pretty kind to you so far. I've not provoked you too much. Here is your first and only quiz of this book. When you hear the word environment, what exactly are you referring to?

Go ahead and answer. It can be a sentence or a collection of words that comes to mind. If this is your book write it here:

_____

_____

_____

_____

I'm not sure what you wrote because we don't yet have instant feedback-to-author technology. Hmmm, I'm adding that to Chapter 13: Compunications. That's not a typo; it is a new word in honor of the future already taking shape, where computers and communications merge.

Okay, back to this chapter and the question about environment. Any answer that includes a variation of "it depends" is excellent.

The environment is the aggregate of surrounding things, conditions, influences, and other factors that affect a given organism. But the key words are "a given organism."

The reason it depends is because it depends on how you frame it. Like the word community you can draw the circle to surround things up close or further away and from a particular point of view.

My work environment is different than your home environment is different than what a farmer would consider their environment. But, what about a bear, a fish or a bee?

We can also talk about the environment surrounding the cells within our body. It is internal to us, but still the external environment from the cell's frame of reference.

Our point of view doesn't change the facts. Something being out of sight might make it out of mind, but that doesn't change the fact that it exists. A tree is still a tree even if we are not looking in the direction of the tree or considering it.

So much of what needs to change in the world is about broadening our perspective.

Before germ theory was accepted, prior to 1880, physicians and scientists believed that diseases such as cholera, Chlamydia or the Black Death were caused by bad air. This was referred to as Miasma theory and was in place since ancient times.

Likewise, at another time in recent history officials banned the word tornado. They didn't want to cause panic. The result was tornadoes still happened of course, and in the absence of warnings, more people and property were unnecessarily harmed, or worse.

When we make things visible we can then actually decide to act differently. If we don't believe in the viruses and bacteria that are invisible to the naked eye then the conversations about preventing infectious diseases are pretty short.

We've progressed too far for people to live in an era of make-believe. If we dispel myths about the environment and better understand the world around us, then we can begin to make decisions that are better for ourselves and the planet we share.

Environment Primer

Our environment includes the social environment, discussed in the previous chapter, the built environment, and the natural environment.

The built environment includes places and spaces that are conceived of and built by humans. The built environment co-exists with nature and includes parks, dams, factories, schools, homes, community gardens, etc. It also includes supporting infrastructure such as water supply and energy networks.

The natural environment, by contrast, is all of the things living and non-living that occur naturally on earth without human involvement. Among these things are natural resources including soil, forests, vegetation, rock, minerals, water, and living organisms. The natural environment also includes things unseen to the naked eye, microorganisms, air, subterranean water, radioactivity, cosmic waves, and electromagnetic and gravitational forces.

Resources in the natural environment can be divided into two distinct groups, renewable and non-renewable.

Minerals, metal ores, fossil fuels (natural gas, coal, and oil) and water in deep aquifers are non-renewable resources. Once extracted and exploited they are gone, forever changed. A natural resource that cannot be replenished on a human time-scale is considered nonrenewable. Fossil fuels are a prime example.

This is unlike timber which if harvested sustainably is a renewable resource. Animal life is also renewable, provided that it is protected and conserved. This applies to animals of the land and sea. Surface water and ground water are renewable resources through the water cycle comprised of precipitation, runoff, infiltration, evaporation, and condensation. Here is how that cycle works.

Precipitation falls in the form of rain or snow. The resulting water or snow melt runs off into streams and rivers, following gravity and also infiltrating the soil. Plants and forests take up the water through their root structures and also accumulate water as precipitation falls on their leaves. Solar radiation from the sun warms water in oceans, rivers, lakes, and soil. As the temperature rises, water molecules move and as the collisions occur some gain enough energy to escape into the air, or evaporate.

Evaporation is the process by which a liquid changes into a vapor. These water vapor molecules move into the atmosphere and form clouds. Water that has been absorbed by plants undergoes a similar evaporative process called transpiration. The transpiration is actually a byproduct of photosynthesis. During the day, plants open tiny pores called stomata (Greek for mouth) taking in carbon dioxide and releasing oxygen. In the process, water vapor is released. These water vapor molecules also contribute to cloud formation.

Rain happens when there are enough condensed atmospheric water vapor molecules that become heavy enough to fall under gravity. The rain then falls depositing fresh water on the natural landscape and the cycle repeats. The rain also falls on the built landscape like hydroelectric power plants and crops. Part of the built landscape is to control how water is held, attenuated (slowed down) diverted, treated, for use and consumption by humans.

Our built environment can either peacefully coexist or invade and overtake the natural environment. If I moved all of the junk in my garage (and I do have some) into your kitchen you'd likely feel crowded. Probably you'd have trouble preparing meals or even accessing your refrigerator. It would upset the balance of living within your home. Well, humans have done this equivalent to the natural environment through deforestation, overgrazing, land degradation, overdevelopment, and releasing chemicals into the air, water, and soil.

Imagine not being able to access your refrigerator, or your stove, or your pantry at all. Your ability to eat and sustain life would be at risk. Collectively, humans are chipping away at the natural resources on the earth that provide us all with life supporting systems.

There are two distinct populations that contribute to critical global environmental problems, but in different ways. The first one is the developed (industrialized) nations that have non-sustainable patterns of consumption and production. These countries consume more of and a wider variety of natural resources than their countries possess. So, they must turn to other countries to fulfill their demand.

The other population responsible for global environmental problems is the developing (non-industrialized) nations. Within these nations people deplete natural resources for their own survival and also to trade with others. Sometimes habitat destruction is inevitable as they have little other alternative.

For example, as the pastoral herdsman turned charcoal entrepreneur, Hussein in Somaliland said, "Each time I cut down a tree, I am left with a bitter taste in my mouth. The future is bleak.... All the trees will have disappeared."[1] Hussein used to keep animals but lost his herd to famine and disease and has now turned to chopping wood to make charcoal in order to feed his family. Sadly this is the plight of many in the developing world, especially rural people. These countries further deplete resources in order to satiate those countries in over consumption mode.

Basic Income. Richer nations providing people like Hussein in developing nations with basic income could turn unintentional environmental assassins into responsible stewards of the earth. Add to that basic income, technical assistance from the Innovation Clearinghouse of Chapter 5, and the human potential expands even further.

What the world needs is a strategy that unites continued economic development with the ongoing preservation of the environment. This strategy is sustainable development, meaning, meeting the needs of the present without compromising the ability of future generations to meet their own needs.[2]

In Chapter 5 we discussed Universal Unconditional Basic Income. There we learned that providing people with basic income is more stable for democracies and produces more customers, more entrepreneurs, and more social good. But, it turns out it is also a way to protect the landscape from further environmental ruin.

You see, things are connected, that chapter and this one, or put another way the economy and the environment. Sustainable development is critically important for all of us.

A Basic Income Grant is an emancipatory measure to enable people to meaningfully participate in a caring and inclusive society. Without economic security, sustainable development is undermined as people like Hussein will resort to whatever measures they need to in order to survive.

Claudia and Dirk Haarmann of the Basic Income Grant (BIG) Coalition are calling on the government of Namibia to provide a Basic Income Grant to all people in the country. This, after successfully executing a Basic Income Grant Pilot in Otjivero that documented positive social and economic impacts of the grant on food security, education, health, crime, and local economic activities.[3] A reference link to the full report is available in the chapter end notes.[4]

Governments are not reacting quickly enough, not in Namibia, nor around the world. Though we all share the same tiny planet, there is still a lack of coordinated political action and responsibility. There has been more political will for trade agreements that are chiefly concerned with the wanton accumulation of resources and more giveaways to multinational corporations than there has been for the rights of people and planet.

It isn't right for humanity, it doesn't scale, and it is destructive to the planet's life supporting systems that we all depend on for survival.

We should declare economic systems that drive the planet toward an unsustainable future, dead. We need to reframe, rethink, and reform. New policies and new conversation are needed. It might also take new politicians and new corporate leaders. Hey, you are a good global citizen; would you like to run for office? If not, at least work your propaganda for good network.

We need to keep constant pressure on our fellow citizens, companies we buy from, and government leaders. We need to ensure they are pursuing policies that work for all people and that they have added nature as a stakeholder. We need a sustainable development equivalent to the Hippocratic Oath, historically taken by physicians.[5]

Imagine corporate and government leaders had a similar oath with lines analogous to these:

- I will remember that I do not treat a fever chart, a

cancerous growth, but a sick human being, whose illness may affect the person's family and economic stability.

- My responsibility includes these related problems, if I am to care adequately for the sick.
- I will prevent disease whenever I can, for prevention is preferable to cure.

The fact that you are reading this book likely places you in one of the over-consuming developed countries. One of the biggest things you can do to contribute to a healthier environment is to reduce your own consumption of natural resources. To do that you'll need to change your view of the world. Some say, the world is shrinking; I say, the world is finite, we become larger.

> **"The real voyage of discovery consists not in seeking new landscapes, but in having new eyes."**
> *Marcel Proust*
> *French Novelist*
> *(1871–1922)*

So aside from reducing food waste as discussed in Chapter 7, what is a person to do? Add to that list unplug, turn off, recycle, compost, and if it is yellow, let it mellow. Seriously, much water is wasted by flushing beemaleem down the toilet. It is brown (boomaloom) then flush it down. According to "Why Flush?," the maker of toilet water neutralizer, the average U.S. household flushes 2000 times per year. With a low flow toilet that is still 4000 gallons of clean, drinkable water. If one percent of U.S. households used "WhyFlush?" we would save billions of gallons of water annually. But, we would also save the related water treatment costs and slow the need to build or expand water treatment plants as populations grow. Less flushing is good.

We don't really think about resources like the water treatment plant because they are mostly invisible to us. Likewise, we use plenty of other resources related to the products and services we consume that are also out of sight and mind.

Think of a chocolate bar you purchase at the store. There were many steps to create that chocolate bar from its original form as cacao beans inside fruit called pods, on a cacao tree somewhere in the tropics, near the equator.

For a chocolate bar, the beans are harvested from the cocoa pods on a tree on a farm or plantation where they are then scraped, wrapped in large green plantain leaves, fermented in the sun, sun dried, sorted, graded, and packed into jute bags. They are then stored in ventilated warehouses until they are transported for sale to a local buyer and then shipped to a processor who then further cleans, roasts, grinds, presses, heats, tempers, moulds and shapes the chocolate for consumption or for reuse in other products as powder.[6] All of these steps consume resources. Add to this more resources needed to package, distribute, advertise, sell, transport, and stock this chocolate bar on the store shelves where you are likely to purchase it.

Ethically and Fair Products. Now, I'm not advocating that you give up your chocolate bar or attempt to grow your own local cacao trees. While you don't have any choice in the steps and resources required to make chocolate, you do have a choice in sourcing Ethically and Fair Products. You can choose to buy from companies concerned with supporting a sustainable and equitable world or from those who are more concerned chiefly with profits, no matter the cost to or plight of others.

When you choose to support fair trade chocolate such as Divine Chocolate, the farmers of Kuapa Kokoo who grow the beans are guaranteed a fair price for their cocoa. This insulates them from the volatility of the market.

From the Divine Chocolate website, "The cooperative receives an additional premium of $200 per tonne, which the cooperative invests in their own projects to improve the farmers' living, health and education standards, and farming productivity. A percentage of the price of Divine goes towards 'producer support and development,' which Kuapa Kokoo spends on farmer education, and helping to maintain the values and vision of the cooperative as it grows. What makes the relationship even more special is that Kuapa co-owns Divine Chocolate Ltd."[7]

In 2011, Kuapa Kokoo teamed up with the International Labor Organization (ILO) to identify, prevent and create awareness on child labor. The cooperative has already highlighted the need for education by building schools where children can prepare for their future while parents work their farms. "If you go to the district now, we have a big school building for the children," said Kuapa Kokoo member and cocoa farmer Felicia Mensah. "Previously, they attended school under a tree, which was very, very bad. So the cooperative has done a lot for the farmers."[8]

By contrast, the film *The Dark Side of Chocolate* reveals another side of chocolate where children as young as seven years old work illegally in the plantation. Many of these kids were illegally trafficked from Mali in West Africa to neighboring Ivory Coast, the world's largest producer of cocoa with more than 40 percent of the world's production.[9] These kids don't attend school under a tree nor anywhere, nor do they speak the local dialect.

You see, things are even more connected when we allow ourselves to see them. Think of who profits the next time you eat your chocolate bar and who might be exploited in the process.

Knowing where our food comes from, how it is processed, who is involved, and who benefits, helps each of us to make more informed decisions about our purchases.

Trace Anything is a comprehensive service that allow purchasers to trace the origin and history of the goods they purchase or intend to purchase. It reveals who is involved in each processing step as well as the materials that are used and their origin. The comprehensive information system and service includes an application and product labeling scheme that is available to shoppers online and in-store. It isn't enough to say a chocolate bar is made in Switzerland; we need to know more. Trace Anything goes beyond food products to include all products from avocados to automobiles.

You may recall a provocative poem written by Pastor Martin Niemöller. There are many versions, the first of which appeared in 1946 after Niemöller was liberated from the concentration camps where he endured the last seven years of Nazi rule. His poem is a powerful statement about the failure of Germans to speak out against the Nazis:

> **"First they came for the Socialists,**
> **and I did not speak out —**
> **Because I was not a Socialist.**
>
> **Then they came for the Trade Unionists,**
> **and I did not speak out —**
> **Because I was not a Trade Unionist.**
>
> **Then they came for the Jews,**
> **and I did not speak out —**
> **Because I was not a Jew.**
>
> **Then they came for me —**
> **and there was no one left to speak for me."**

Fredrick Gustav Emil Martin Niemöller
German anti-Nazi theologian, Lutheran pastor
President, World Council of Churches (1961–1968)
(1892–1984)

Niemöller believed that Germans — in particular the leaders of the Protestant churches — had been complicit through their silence in the Nazi imprisonment, persecution, and murder of millions of people.[10]

Whether it is children and chocolate, bees and pesticides, or trees and charcoal, we cannot pretend it doesn't matter merely because it isn't in our own neighborhood or hemisphere.

Niemöller's poem could easily be modernized to reflect others exploited and forgotten: unemployed and underemployed, victims of human trafficking, economic and war refugees or even polar bears. The point of course is we must act together and prevent "oxygen deprived humans" from joining the list. We must heighten our collective consciousness and be more mindful in the decisions we make and let others make on our behalf.

If we produce less things that the world doesn't need, it will preserve resources. This has become an obvious fact throughout history as countries at war routinely reused goods, rationed, and recycled materials. But, we needn't be at war to learn from this or mobilize people to protect all resources, for all nations. Let's stop using valuable resources to create things and then bury them in landfills when we tire of them or they break, often prematurely.

Fix Anything Attendant. No matter whether a product is a printer, a chair, garden umbrella, computer, or a pair of pants, whenever it breaks or stops functioning, bring it to the Fix Anything Attendant. These people can fix most anything. They will also collect information from each repair so that it can be provided to manufacturers to inform product design. Fix Anything Attendants are in every region, but they share a global network and knowledge base.

Drop off your product. Pick it up later. No more

sending fixable products to the landfill because there isn't a repair center. If you no longer want the product then it can be 100 percent sustainably recycled or put to use by another person.

The Fix Anything Attendant is beneficial to customers, but the network also serves as "sensors in the ground" for manufactures. Each manufacture becomes aware of what repairs were made by the Fix Anything Attendant. Solutions are shared on a global knowledge network. Enough information collected from enough attendants and designers are better able to improve product design, identify faulty materials in their supply chains, and better understand usage patterns. Of course, they still have to want to improve.

Some products are artificially affordable because the real costs are externalized to the public. This includes the wasted resources in the creation of the product, but also in its premature disposal which further consumes resources.

Junk Tax. For those products deemed junk and of a temporary nature, let's institute a Junk Tax or landfill tax to help offset the actual costs to society. This tax can help to fund environmental restoration projects and awareness.

In similar fashion, products that are designed to have long life spans, be 100 percent recyclable, and have reusable components, will qualify for favorable tax status.

Buy Once Label. One of the byproducts of a fix anything movement would be a strive to produce higher quality goods that are repairable or even upgradeable.

Imagine a Buy Once Label, seal, or certification earned by those products that don't suffer recalls, are not thrown away, and do not routinely show up at the Fix Anything Attendant. Though this label would be extraordinary today and the product remarkable this should by design become the way of the world.

New Standards For Design And Manufacturing would value the resources of the planet. Part of those standards would be the message that is carried with every manufactured product. Among other things, the label would indicate that this product can be: upgraded, repaired, returned for credit or reuse, composted, or recycled.

The next Industrial Revolution is already underway. This one is different than the last one in that it has values.

The European Commission, the EU's executive body, recently released a draft circular economy package. Policymakers believe that the shift to a circular economy, in which as little is wasted as possible, is necessary in a world with finite resources and a booming population.[11] The paper is not yet finalized. It does include provisions of eco-design which aim to make products more energy and resource efficient. It currently falls short of demanding that products be upgradeable or repairable, but that will come.

Though many policy makers have been slow to respond, there are groups that are empowering individuals and communities to rethink superfluous waste and our relationship with the earth's resources.

Zero Waste Europe. One such group, Zero Waste Europe, would like to see anything that can't be repaired, composted or recycled instead be re-designed and replaced or banned from entering the market.[12]

Cradle to Cradle Innovation Institute. The Cradle to Cradle Innovation Institute is doing their part to educate and empower designers and manufacturers, providing them with a framework to improve products across five sustainability factors: material health; material reutilization; renewable energy and carbon management; water stewardship; and social fairness. Qualifying products are awarded one of five levels of achievement — Basic, Bronze, Silver, Gold, or Platinum.[13]

Manufacturer PUMA's InCycle collection of products has been certified by the Cradle to Cradle Products Innovation Institute. All materials in the collection are either biodegradable, industrial compostable, or recyclable.

In similar fashion Puma has created the "Bring Me Back" program where people bring in used shoes, clothing and accessories from any manufacture to a PUMA store and deposit them in the "Bring Me Back" bins. The products are then sent off to be re-used if still in suitable condition or recycled into new raw materials and products. This gives people an easy way to lessen their environmental impact.[14]

More and more, concerned citizens of the planet and the companies they power are going to provide people with authentic product choices that are healthy, safe, and sustainable. We can all choose to reduce our individual carbon footprint.

But, individuals need to be organized and mobilized to make an even bigger impact. And that is still the domain of governments, especially when it comes to the physical realm where the digital giants don't yet roam.

As U.S. President Abraham Lincoln once said, "Government should do for people what people cannot do for themselves."

It has been governments that historically invested in funding heavy infrastructure we've come to rely on in the built environment. Bridges, sewers, and water mains come to mind. But, the U.S. federal government, in particular, has also funded agencies and federal laboratories that have created many of the things we take for granted in our daily lives — conveniences such as the Internet, cell phones, microprocessors that are embedded in everything from cars to toasters, even many of our medical treatments and drugs.

If you think about it, government funded research is the original crowdfunding system. The difference is that individuals didn't visit a website, use a credit card, or choose which project to invest in. Instead, the way it works is that taxpayers provide money to the federal government by paying taxes. Then, the federal government authorizes funding through various funding mechanisms to various agencies and federally funded research and development centers.

The Arpanet, the predecessor to the Internet, was run for 20 years as a U.S. Department of Defense project, until 1990. Since then the Internet and World Wide Web has blossomed. And, so have the applications, content, and services that sit on top of the internetwork of computers.

Today we have cyber espionage, hackers, scammers, spoofers, and a host of other fraudsters, trolls, and electronic denizens.

But, imagine we worked together and put those creative forces to good use. That is the world in which we all want to live. First it will be thousands, then millions, and then billions and pretty soon we'll not need to spend enormous amounts of money on defense and weapons. That would be pointless. After all, why would we want to harm our shared community?

When we work together we accomplish much more. I imagine a world where the U.S. the EU and China collaborate on research and innovation and the Innovation Clearinghouse freely moves talents and resources to accomplish meaningful projects. Add to that the Middle East, Russia, Africa and keep going. Really, there is no justification to leave any people of any nation out. We all share the same tiny planet.

Greed keeps countries and corporations from sharing with others and fear prevents them from taking collaborative risks. Instead they invest in protecting themselves, the figurative equivalent of building fences. In fact, you've seen this happen literally in some Eastern European countries to redirect "those immigrants" (refugees) from entering their countries. Some U.S.

politicians and corporate leaders would like to build a fence similarly. Nationalistic tendencies are opposing humanistic actions in Europe as leaders attempt to welcome refugees.

But, imagine we were freed from greed and fear. Imagine the possibilities if we leveraged all talent.

Our combined efforts could be spending our research and innovation dollars in the area of environment to create a better built environment and to restore and protect the natural landscape.

First, we need one view of the truth. We need to dispense with pretense and secrets. Instead, we need transparency and shared data.

Remember the Truth Sculpture of Chapter 5? It is important that we have facts and data about the environment.

China has killed their pollinators and now they rely on hand pollination. Meanwhile, in the U.S. people are divided over what is decimating domestic honeybee populations. Some say it is the Asian mite, others attribute it to natural causes (bees are always dying), and still others claim pesticides like neonictides are to blame.

Well, let's talk to the Chinese agriculture experts and learn from their mistakes. Then let's surface the facts and build a Truth Sculpture. Don't worry if you work for a pesticide manufacture and ultimately lose your job. People of the future actually care about *people* so the social safety net will help you land another job, or even a career.

Facts and data are great. A Truth Sculpture is a splendid thing. But, it isn't exactly preventative.

Ecosystem Monitor Alert (EMA). In order to prevent damage from occurring we need another innovation, an Ecosystem Monitor Alert (EMA).

Sensor technology has evolved to where we can monitor birds in flights, quality of air and water, movement of tectonic plates, tsunamis, and just about anything else we wish to monitor. Along with that we have remote communications capabilities that enable us to extract sensor data from even the most remote areas. So, let's put sensors in fragile ecosystems and monitor them so they are not out of sight and out of mind. Let's detect when the balance of nature becomes upset and then send alerts to communities, organizations, authorities, and other stakeholders — our collective culture of care.

Technology is great, but it's complimentary to humans who have sensors, too. Real people can walk around, enter places and spaces, look around and into objects, talk to others, ask questions, investigate, explore, and use their senses of sight, taste, touch, smell, and hearing. Beyond observing and investigating, humans can operate equipment, record, recall, communicate, and if necessary wave a Norm Flag, even declare a System Reset.

While Norm Flags are appropriate for those stakeholders inside an organization we need the ability from the outside to take similar action, to be able to say, "Hey something is not quite right here."

Surface This is exactly that mechanism with the added benefit of amplification. Many times media organizations are self interested and fail to cover a story that is relevant to an unknowing public. Surface This works in conjunction with the Propaganda for Good Network. Global citizens in the network stand at the ready to communicate and amplify Ecosystem Monitor Alerts or other messages not being conveyed by mainstream media. The same mechanism can also work to counter false stories or gather sentiment for issues important to the public such as the Pots and Pans Revolution in Iceland or the desire to once again make legal in the U.S., growing agricultural hemp for its many medicinal, industrial, and culinary benefits.

We have brilliant people in the world. Together, let's ask new questions. And then find the answers and share solutions. If we can do this on an International Space Station, surely we can do it on earth.

Countries Cooperate in Space, Why Not on Earth?

Astronaut Ron Garan and author of *The Orbital Perspective: Lessons in Seeing the Big Picture from a Journey of 71 Million Miles*, offers an interesting perspective, one that he reflected on from 100 feet above the International Space Station while on a space walk.

"What really struck me in that moment was the international cooperation that built the International Space Station. When you look at the difference between the beauty of our planet and the unfortunate realities of life on our planet, it makes you wonder."

He went on to say, "If we could do that in space — fifteen nations, several of which were not always the best of friends, some of which were on the opposite sides of the Cold War, opposite sides of the space race — if they could do that in space, imagine what we could do by working together to solve the problems facing our planet."[15]

Imagine governments providing policy that embraces our common humanity and focuses people on advancing human progress. Imagine policies that spark innovation and investments that fund innovation. We can have progress while protecting natural resources and protecting human rights. Imagine further innovations and human progress in the following areas:

- Harvesting energy already around us
- Innovating new energy systems
- Creating protections from effects of climate change
- Improving the landscape
- Innovating inside our homes

Harvesting Energy Already Around Us

Let's make use of the energy that is already in place. Fossil fuels that originated as crude oil deep within the earth were not used by humans, that is, until they were. Likewise, we can make new choices about other potential sources of energy.

The use of fossil fuels didn't even make sense until the Industrial Revolution. The steam engine and electric generator came in close proximity and further fueled factories, transportation, and eventually what became to be our consumer life. Gottlieb Daimler created the first practical automobile engine that ran off of gasoline and ushered in an era of transportation of all types that evolved to make use of fossil fuels and fossil fuel infrastructure.

But, fuels we depend upon to heat homes, power engines, and industry don't have to come from crude oil. It turns out that we can and do make fuel using biomass products. Just as we have created petroleum based refineries we can choose to create biomass oriented refineries. More on that later in this chapter.

We have plenty of water on the earth's surface and it's growing. Yes, that is correct. As the planet warms sea levels rise. Aside from the melting of land-based ice, as the planet warms it also warms the oceans, causing them to thermally expand.

And, the moon isn't going away. So let's leverage these two natural resources that work together to create predictable, useable tides.

Tidal Power Plants. We have very few Tidal Power Plants on the entire earth. We can do much better. Let's learn from La Rance Tidal Power Plant in France that has been in continuous operation since 1966.[16] The fully renewable power plant generates enough annual output to serve the needs of approximately 130,000 homes every year. Similar technology was deployed for tidal mills since the

Roman times. Some of those are still standing today.

Harvest Wave Energy. As waves continuously crash into breakwaters, jetties, seawalls, and other structures let's have the water spin turbines to generate electricity.

Carnegie Wave Energy among others have been running pilots to harness wave motion for renewable energy. Carnegie's approach is a submerged buoy system; others are using other approaches.[17] While the approach might be different, ultimately they all produce clean renewable energy.

One innovative company, Lucid Energy, is helping cities to turn their water pipelines into generators of carbon-free renewable energy.[18] Other companies are using similar technologies to turn tidal currents into electricity.[19]

All of these projects are at the early stages and represent clean energy that doesn't add to carbon emissions.

Just as governments funded nuclear research, we need investments in wave energy systems, too. As the Chief Executive of Carnegie Wave Systems of Perth, Australia said, "The biggest challenge is funding. Any power generation product is capital-intensive. Anytime you want to test an idea, it costs millions of dollars. Energy technologies that are mainstream today, like nuclear power, were developed for commercial use with government research and support."

Rainwater Impellers. Imagine similar energy harvesting technology on a smaller scale for use in homes, perhaps in gutters and downspouts, on the way to the storm water systems that could have similar harvesting technology.

In the future when a rainy city such as Ketchikan, Alaska, Portland, Oregon or Seattle, Washington gets soaked by a downpour, it will have residents and meteorologists skipping the rain gauge, and instead focusing on the kilowatts of rain-produced renewable energy.

[I've added this section in brackets for emphasis. Here is why. Though I was currently working in another section of the book, I was compelled to revisit the Rainwater Impeller impossible idea. For a couple of days now, in Seattle, we've been deluged with rain. I'm looking out my window right now, watching water flowing over paved surfaces making its way to stormwater systems and eventually out to streams and rivers already at flood stage. I can't help but think of all of the energy that is wasted in this water cycle and every water cycle. Scientist and engineers have long been damming rivers to get hydropower, but we've not yet made even tiny amounts of progress when it comes to homes, neighborhoods, and communities, which taken together is all of us. Entrepreneurs reading this — are you listening?]

Innovating New Energy Systems
At one point in human history we had no energy systems, no electricity, not even simple machines like the lever. It was Archimedes who first conceived of simple machines. Archimedes lived during tumultuous times. He was killed by a Roman soldier at 75 years of age. Although Archimedes invented the underpinning of integral calculus during his lifetime (287 BC–212 BC) it wouldn't be rediscovered in full until the 16th century during the Renaissance. Imagine the progress human civilization could have made had Archimedes not been killed. All of the things described in this book probably would have already happened by now.

Energy Turf is artificial grass that appears as normal grass, but it is a tiny network of energy producers. Each time the tiny blades are deflected by wind or by foot, they convert mechanical energy into electrical energy. Individual blades acts like the delicate hairs of the cochlea inside the human ear. In the ear, waves of sound deflect delicate hairs which in turn convert this movement into nerve impulses which are then carried to the brain by the auditory nerve. The brain decodes the information and we "hear" a sound.

In the case of Energy Turf, when blades are deflected a tiny amount of electrical energy is produced. The tiny electrical contribution of each blade, taken together over a small field or patch of grass, on a windy day (or a day of child's play), can add up to a relevant amount of energy. This energy can be used locally to power outdoor lights or be placed back on the power grid with micro power conditioners. Best of all, Energy Turf consumes no water, never needs mowing and is green both in color and in energy.

Energy Plant is similar to Energy Turf in that it is artificial and creates green energy. But, Energy Plant is the upright varietal that has more exposure to the wind, solar, and thermal energy given its branch and leaf structure. Energy Plant can also be used as a water harvester during periods of rain or dew.

Microgrid Connect. In the future there will be more locally generated power than the common scenario of centralized bulk energy creation. Capturing energy via multiple methods at their source, e.g., local wind, wave, solar, etc., makes good sense. It takes advantage of otherwise unharvested energy and reduces the amount of centralized energy creation needed, energy production that may not be clean. Locally produced energy provides security and independence to communities, businesses and even nations.

With the right investments and technology smallholder created energy can be less expensive and uncomplicated.

Microgrid Connect takes the complexity out of connecting to the power grid. This become as easy in the future as establishing an Internet connection today.

Gridport is a new type of electrical outlet where you plug in small-scale energy harvesting devices. Gridport is available for every home and business. If more energy is created than consumed, the excess energy can be stored locally or provided back onto the community power grid.

> **"Only those who attempt the absurd**
> **will achieve the impossible.**
> **I think it's in my basement ...**
> **let me go upstairs and check."**
>
> *Maurits Cornelis Escher*
> *Dutch artist most famous for his so-called*
> *impossible constructions*
> *(1989–1972)*

Creating Protections From Effects of Climate Change

Gravity still affects you even if you don't believe in it. The climate has been changing; it is observable, it is measurable. Many people who continue to deny these facts have a bias for tradition. They simply don't want to hear of a carbon neutral economy, or transition from the old ways. Put more simply, they probably materially gain and find convenience in a fossil fuel based economy.

As John Kerry said in a recent acceptance speech while receiving the diplomat of the year award, "On climate change, the good news is the momentum is building. Around the globe, mayors and governors are getting involved, civil society is mobilizing, religious authority is weighing in, the private sector is opening a whole new green frontier. So the time has come, frankly, to bring the former skeptics into the fold. There is nothing liberal or conservative, nothing republican or democratic, there is nothing global north or global south about the potential consequences of climate change. We all have the same stake because we all share the same fragile home."

Even if someone doesn't believe in climate change or that man-made actions have contributed to it, you have to be in serious denial to not see that climate change has negatively affected other people.

As sea levels rise they swallow up shorelines and the coastal and island communities. Residents of Newtok, Alaska are finding their land literally disappearing due to rising water and the erosive power of tides and storm surges that sweep their land out to sea and leave areas of the treeless turf covered in water — areas where residents formerly gathered berries and hunted moose.

According to a recent report by the U.S. Government Accountability Office, 184 of Alaska's 213 native villages are threatened by erosion, thirty-one of them in imminent danger of total collapse. And those numbers grow every year.[20]

Still worse, the plight of an eroded or submerged future isn't limited to natives of Alaska. Residents of the Maldives, an archipelago of coral islands off the southern tip of India, face the same situation. So do those in the Kiribati, Tokelau, and Tuvalu, the tiny island nations located in the middle of the Pacific Ocean about halfway between Hawaii and New Zealand. These are among the most remote places on Earth, the equivalent of deep in the jungle, but in this case, the ocean. The inhabitants of these islands are out of sight and out of mind for most people in developed nations.

Ghoramara Island in the bay of Bengal has already lost over half of its land mass to rising sea water and floods. People who once cultivated land and grew vegetables are no longer able to do so as saline water renders their land inhospitable. Many convert to becoming fisherman in already crowded waters. Because the future is bleak, still others leave to begin a new life elsewhere.[21]

A new life elsewhere is possible for those residents of

the Marshall Islands. Marshallese people are able to migrate to the U.S. easily because of the Compact Of Free Association. In the exchange for the United States being able to keep a military base on one of the islands, people are able to work in the U.S. without a visa.[22]

This shows the possibilities to help when there is interest. So let's create more interest for the climate refugees of the planet, wherever they are and before they are submerged.

A former nonprofit client whose organization serves women experiencing homelessness, once shared with me the concern of a woman who came to her for help. She said, "Why do I have to lose everything, in order to get some help?"

There is no endangered species act for humans, at least not yet. Imagine there was a constituency for climate refugees, before they became climate refugees. Let's help people, before they are swimming in the ocean, whether or not we have a military base there or other economic interests. As human beings we have a moral responsibility to other human beings.

Transferring Funds and Technology. We should help people in place by Transferring Funds and Technology to build up, maintain and protect or improve their built environment. In some cases, with technical training and capacity building, the ecological balance can be restored, protecting people from the natural environment. The Innovation Clearinghouse has the talent and resources to help restore fragile ecosystems. Like Doctors Without Borders, we have scientists, engineers, construction workers, and whatever else is needed (also without borders) standing by ready and willing to assist.

Restore the Ecological Balance. When possible let's Restore the Ecological Balance in places that have suffered under the hands of human "progress."

When the enormity of the task is cost prohibitive or ecologically unsound, let's declare a System Reset. The coast of England and Wales is being eroded by waves. The Environment Agency estimates that 7000 properties will be sacrificed to rising seas in the next century, 800 in the next 20 years. At stake is more than £1 billion worth of properties. The cost of protecting these properties is deemed to be too high.[23] So, let's relocate people and repurpose the border between the built environment and the natural landscape. Instead of waterfront homes and businesses perhaps we should build a wave energy harvester that serves all people with clean energy.

Relocate People. Whether people are in developed nations or developing nations, if they are soon to be climate refugees let's relocate them and share the blessings and burdens of doing so.

Conventional scorecard measures for this might look like a losing proposition, but the humanity scorecard would value the efforts highly.

You can't hide climate change. As more human beings are displaced physically or become economic refugees because their means of economic support are damaged the issue will become more visible.

In the future, an engaged global citizenry will become increasingly demanding of their leaders to take action and create real policies to address environmental degradation and to provide assistance to people.

But, humans on the whole, don't seem to be very good students of human history. The dust bowl in the Midwest that John Steinbeck famously portrayed in, *The Grapes of Wrath* is being replayed today. California is creating another dust bowl today.

Other areas either unknowingly harm their environment or have little choice given poor economic alternatives. As the pastoral herdsman turned charcoal entrepreneur, Hussein in Somaliland said, "Each time I cut down a tree, I am left with a bitter taste in my mouth.... The future is bleak. All the trees will have disappeared."[24]

"An ounce of prevention is worth a pound of cure."

Benjamin Franklin
Author, printer, political theorist,
politician, freemason, postmaster,
scientist, inventor, civic activist, statesman,
and diplomat.
(1706–1790)

Other solutions in this book, working together, address prevention and when implemented, serve to reduce human caused climate disruptions. But, the damage is already in motion for some areas and for the people who inhabit them. So, let's put protections in place, to lessen continued damage, to people and property.

Fire Killing Oxygen Depletion Blanket. Wild fires (either field or forest) can get out of hand quickly as winds fan flames and blow burning embers to surrounding fuel sources. Fires need the presence of heat, fuel, and oxygen to continue burning. Remove any one of those and the fire goes out. Firefighters have successfully used fire blankets to smother small fires for as long as they've been fighting fires.

So, imagine this at a much larger scale. For large burns imagine four specially design helicopters flying in formation, carrying a common payload beneath them, a large Fire Killing Oxygen Depletion Blanket.

Once the helicopters are in place, the crew chief remotely triggers the drop. Each of the helicopters release the payload in unison. The blanket falls to the tree tops, covers the forest canopy immediately stopping the spread of wind-blown embers. At the edges of the blanket are multiple fire bots each of which rappels to the forest floor.

Fire Resistant Robots. A Fire Resistant Robot's job is to pull the blanket taught to the forest floor. Each robot winds the cable and signals the blanket that it has completed it pull. When all signals have been received the blanket automatically initiates oxygen suck. It extracts the oxygen under the blanket evacuating it skyward. The blanket can be left in place while the fire burns elsewhere or retrieved immediately and reused, unlike fire retardant and water drops which are single use.

For smaller burns that need to be extinguished, instead of helicopters, a cannon propelled version can be used. Affix the cannon side of the blanket to the ground and launch the blanket skyward across a burning field, or over trees or other obstacles. The same principles apply. Cinch the sides and watch the fire get smothered.

Residents of hilly regions, where fires have decimated their forest and brush, face a new danger, mudslides. When rains come and there isn't anything to stop it, it will form erosive rivers that soften hillside and indiscriminately send torrents of mud into homes, highways, and whatever else is in the path.

Biomimicry. Nature is an excellence designer. Biomimicry is the practice of designing by learning from nature. It turns out, nature is the original hacker. Mother Nature has been at it for a very long time, much longer than humans have been designing anything.

So, when we wish to solve a problem, we should first consult nature. You can actually, thanks to the many collaborators at AskNature.org, a project spawned by the Biomimicry Institute. AskNature provides innovators with the world's most comprehensive catalog of nature's solutions to human design challenges.

As humans have erected buildings and paved streets and other surfaces we've altered the natural flow of water and the balance around it. Runoff occurs when more rain falls than what the earth is able to absorb during any given duration. Too much runoff and soil can become degraded through erosion, creating sediment in other areas. In urban areas runoff can overwhelm storm sewer systems and significantly increase pollutants carried into streams, rivers, and lakes. These pollutants include pesticides, fertilizers, oil, grease, toxic chemicals from motor vehicles, heavy metals, and trash. Water quality suffers and aquatic life is harmed. The impervious asphalt and concrete cover in a typical city creates five times the runoff of a typical woodland of the same size.[25]

Nature solves this problem by a combination of solutions to collect, store, absorb and attenuate water i.e., slow it down, thereby reducing kinetic, and potentially erosive energy. How does nature do this?

Roots from trees and other vegetation bind the soil and soak up water. The canopy of leaves breaks downpours of rain into gentle showers. Downed timber and succulents further absorb water before letting what remains percolate groundcover, infiltrate the soil, and contribute to the water stored underground in aquifers. Aquifers act as reservoirs for groundwater.

Flood Sponge Tree. Imagine a nature inspired Flood Sponge Tree. The tree could be deployed to flood ravaged areas or "planted" for preventative measures. The "timber" of the Flood Sponge Tree would soak up water and rise into a giant stable structure.

Absorptive Wormlike Tubes. An alternative structure is in the form of a giant Absorptive Wormlike Tube. This would especially be useful in the fire damaged areas that are then prone to mudslides.

Whichever structure, these water collecting and storage devices bloat as they collect water and then automatically reduce in size, releasing water over time, as local conditions improve. Warning to low flying aircraft — beware of rapidly rising sponge trees.

Of course, where we can, we should simply leverage nature's gifts and plant water absorbing, pollution filtering, soil protecting, oxygen giving, shelter providing, glorious, and all natural trees.

Planting trees is good for the planet as trees absorb carbon dioxide, one of the gases that collect in the atmosphere, trap heat, and warm the planet. Trees are good for people too, with many positive psychological benefits.

Being in the presence of swaying trees reduces anxiety, lowers blood pressure and connects us to the natural environment.[26] The soothing rhythmic motion of trees or even grass is not unlike that of mothers who instinctively use gentle swaying motion to comfort their babies. Did you ever notice that you feel better around trees or in a rocking chair?

"The symbolism — and the substantive significance — of planting a tree has universal power in every culture and every society on Earth, and it is a way for individual men, women and children to participate in creating solutions for the environmental crisis."

Albert Arnold "Al" Gore, Jr.
45th Vice President of the United States
Author, environmental activist,
2007 Nobel Peace Prize Winner
(born March 31, 1948)

Trees are a generous gift from nature. Humans can be generous designers as well.

Generous Design

As I describe in *The Experience Design Blueprint*, generous design makes people smile. When an organization exceeds expectations without any pressure to do so, people often take notice. It might mean going beyond what is required by law or code, or even the norm set by competitors. Often the thoughtfulness goes unnoticed, but the design still serves to make things a little easier or a little better.

When you see generous design firsthand you think to yourself, "Wow, somebody thought of that. How nice!" But, more importantly you feel that somebody cared and as a result they touched your heart and your mind. Generous design goes beyond expectations, like a dual drinking station for humans and canines alike or a stair rail that extends a little more than required, so that it comfortably greets those about to meet the stairs. Unexpected trees alongside the built environment can be generous gifts that restore the human spirit, cause us to slow down, and even provide healing. We see and feel these in urban areas, parks, boulevards, universities, and even healthcare facilities.

The coastal city of Zadar in Croatia was left devastated following the Second World War. The stone peninsula, was the headquarters of a German garrison that was incessantly bombed by British and American planes. Reconstruction following the end of the war turned the sea wall into a monotonous unwelcoming concrete wall, that is until 2004 when reconstruction began to support the arrival of cruise ships.[27] Concrete has now given way to large slabs of white marble that gently emerge from the Adriatic sea, welcoming new arrivals. Beneath the slabs of marble, lies a series of channels that connect to 35 organ pipes.

As wind and waves push air through the channel, nature made musical compositions emerge from the steps for all to hear. The experimental musical instrument, Morske Orgulje, or the Sea Organ of Zadar is the generous design of architect Nikola Bašić.[28] The showpiece on the seaside promenade welcomes arrivals and is also where families, lovers and friends assemble for what Alfred Hitchcock claimed to be the most beautiful sunset in the world.[29] If the sights aren't beautiful enough for you, the sound of the sea interacting with the organ might compel you to add the Sea Organ of Zadar to your bucket list. See the end notes for a link to a recording.[30]

Improving the Landscape

While we are working on the environment let's fix the blight on many urban landscapes beginning with abandoned shopping carts, those carts taken from store property then left abandoned to litter the landscape at bus stops, on sidewalks and other places in many developed areas.

Obedient Cart solves the abandoned shopping cart problem. Now, as you arrive inside a grocery store, you can select a companion cart that will then pleasantly roll alongside you. Obedient Cart dutifully shops with you, and upon command, proceeds to checkout. When ready, the cart accompanies you to your vehicle, bus stop, or home. Once unpaired, obedient cart's duty is to return to the home store or another in the vicinity where it's most needed. The self driving carts obey traffic laws and signals, travel on sidewalks where available, and cross at crosswalks.

This impossible idea could have easily appeared in the Food & Comfort or Transportation chapters, but it is here since abandoned shopped carts sit stranded, a huge source of conflict in the landscape.

Stores don't want to prosecute customers, nor do they want the expense of replenishing carts. City councils and police want to hold store owners accountable and don't appreciate the liability posed by carts on public streets and sidewalks. And, citizens and business owners grow weary of seeing the urban landscape littered with abandoned carts and the litter they often attract.

Noise from vehicles is a modern annoyance, especially for those living near highways. Traffic noise abatement has taken the form of large walls, usually made of concrete or wood. In the past these walls didn't offer any additional benefit to drivers or residents living nearby.

Energy Harvesting Highway System. The Energy Harvesting Highway System busily collects and stores energy, much like a harried squirrel collecting and storing nuts for food over the winter.

Walls, barriers, bridges, and even the roadway surface become host to myriad micro-scale energy harvesting technologies. Solar cells embedded in surfaces convert sunlight into electrical energy. Similarly, a continuous grid of tiny sensors in roadways collects energy from the vibration and compression under vehicle tires.[31]

All of the solar and mechanical energy converted to electrical energy is cumulatively stored. Over time and distance the efforts of the small scale energy harvesters adds up to a significant amount of energy that can then be used locally (off grid) for lighting, communications, or pollution control.

With the help of an additional ally, energy harvested from highways can be used to fight carbon dioxide (CO_2) pollution caused by gas-powered vehicles. The transportation sector is the second largest source of anthropogenic (human generated) carbon dioxide emissions, behind electricity and heat generation. Road transport accounts for 72 percent of the transportation sector's carbon dioxide emissions.[32]

The unlikely ally in this pollution fight is algae, already the source of much of Earth's oxygen, living in the ocean as well as freshwater systems. Energy harvested from highways can power nearby filters and pumps in a closed loop algae farm designed to eat carbon dioxide emitted from tailpipes. Photosynthesizing algae consume the carbon dioxide as well as sunlight and in exchange provide fresh oxygen.

Carbon Sucking Algae. Like trees, algae absorb CO2 and sunlight and convert it to oxygen through photosynthesis. But microalgae organisms are considered ten times more efficient than trees or grass when it comes to photosynthesis.

Aside from cleaning up our pollution, as algae matures the living biomass can be harvested and used to create clean biofuels.

Algae Biofuels contain no sulfur, are non-toxic and are biodegradable. A number of algae strains produce fuel with energy densities comparable to those of conventional (fossil) fuels. They are made from a renewable resource that is carbon neutral: the emissions that result from burning the fuel are balanced by the absorption of CO2 by the growing organisms.[33] Everybody wins — people and planet.

Microalgae are capable of producing 30 times the amount of oil per unit area of land, compared to terrestrial oilseed crops.

Unlike other crops used for biofuels, alga based biofuel doesn't contribute to deforestation, nor does it compete with agriculture systems. And since sea borne algae can thrive in the ocean, they don't compete for freshwater resources either.

As the U.S. Department of Energy's Office of Fuels Development concluded in their 1998 report, "Microalgae are remarkable and efficient biological factories capable of taking a waste (zero-energy) form of carbon (CO_2) and converting it into a high density liquid form of energy (natural oil)." From 1978 to 1996, the U.S. Department of Energy's Office of Fuels Development funded a program to develop renewable transportation fuels from algae.[34]

Deriving energy from algal biomass is attractive in that unlike fossil fuels, algal biomass is rather uniformly distributed over much of the earth's surface, and its utilization makes no net contribution to increasing atmospheric CO_2 levels.[35]

Not only does this make sense for the environment, it makes good economic sense. Much of the costs related to exploration, transportation, and redistribution of petrochemical fuels aren't required for locally produced Algal Biofuels. Not only is it less expensive and cleaner burning, but it makes oil spills a purely historic phenomenon. And, if an oil spill were to occur, it would be harmless.

If those reasons weren't enough, it also makes good energy security policy for nations.

As smart companies and countries invest in sustainable solutions, you'll see this slimy, pollution sucking companion whirling along in roadside tubes and on overpasses unknowingly contributing to a more sustainable future for its human allies.

Closer To Home
In the future, once we return home from our self driving transportation pods or algae biofueled vehicles, we're likely to encounter other innovations friendly to people and planet.

Sentient Light Bulbs sense people in the room as well as ambient lighting. If more intense lighting is preferred using a "lights up" gesture will increase the intensity. Change the mood in a room by dimming the lighting using a "lights down" gesture. People sensing light bulbs communicate across the network of fixtures and bulbs lighting the room as you enter, dimming and turning off lights as you leave. Teenagers leaving lights on becomes a things of the past.

Security mode allows for timed sequences and panic mode fully illuminates all lights on the network.

Bug Escape. Unless it is a lucky lady bug, insects inside a house are unwelcome and offer no benefit. Bug Escape is the intelligent bug screen that upon detecting bugs on the inside of a window screen, gives them easy egress. No more sun baked dead bugs on the inside of the window. No longer will bees and flies exhaustively search in vain for an exit to the outside. Bug Escape equipped window screens automatically open a portion of the window screen to allow bugs to escape without incident and without human intervention. You're welcome bugs (and humans).

Solar Harvesting Comfort Windows (SHC). Power the Bug Escape window screen, motorized blinds or shades, or other devices by reusing the energy collected from Solar Harvesting Comfort Windows (SHC). Fully transparent solar cells make every window a power source.[36] Programmable and sensing properties of the window enable it to preserve comfort and save energy. SHC windows allow heat to pass through from the outside, but only if the temperature of the room needs additional thermal energy. If the room is at the desired thermostatically set temperature, then SHC windows block external thermal energy from entering the room, a very useful feature on a hot summer day. SHC windows maintain lighting in the room and are able to collect solar energy, whether they are in passing or blocking mode.

Chapter Summary

Phew, you got through it. That was a longer chapter than the rest. You are a good global citizen and student. I hope you learned much about the environment and broadened your perspective.

Impossible ideas around the environment will become less so in the future as climate change becomes more personal for each and every person on the planet.

With so many of us on the planet, even our little choices add up to make a big difference. Whether we are rewarding the label that reflects good values when choosing a product for purchase, bringing a broken product into a repair facility, or providing space in our home for a climate displaced refugee, these decisions move humanity in the right direction.

But, all of our collective desires and efforts across the network of global citizens will be in vain if political leaders set policy that crushes energy innovation, retards human progress, and pushes civilizations toward extinction. So, let's not let that happen.

"Only to the white men was nature a 'wilderness' and only to him was the land 'infested' with 'wild' animals and 'savage' people. To us it was tame. Earth was bountiful and we were surrounded with the blessing of the Great Mystery."

Luther Standing Bear
Native American author,
educator, philosopher, and actor
(1868–1939)

With seven billion people on the planet and growing, we might not ever return to the holistic and respectful nature that Luther understood and espoused.

But, we can be more mindful of how our actions and decisions interact with the other living organisms on the planet, whether those are bees or other human beings.

We need a new political agenda that favors humans and the planet, both of which are increasingly under siege. In the next chapter, we'll explore an upgrade to our political operating system.

10 POLITICS & CRIME

How fitting that these two subject go together. Too much public policy really isn't about the public at all. It merely serves special interests. In the future we'll need to upgrade our political operating system to tip the favor toward humans and the environment. Its game over for some, but game just beginning for others — many that were never before even invited to play.

The Original Lawyers. Sophists were the original lawyers. Schooled in the art of manipulating language they have little regard for anything other than winning. That was the game they played. They were master of all things oratory. The legal profession began when sophists began taking money for their services.

It's not that law is bad. It's that law has little to do with the truth or facts. And, that's a problem because when some lawyers win, all of us lose.

Case in point, hemp. The U.S. Government and hemp have had an on-again, off-again relationship. At times throughout history, authorities have encouraged farmers to grow hemp. During certain periods it was actually illegal to NOT grow hemp. But, at other times, U.S. policy towards hemp was fixated on demonizing the plant that had been associated with its intoxicating cousin, marijuana.[1]

Botanically speaking, the two plants are related in that they are both members of the cannabis family. But, chemically, hemp is very different from marijuana. The fact is you couldn't get high from hemp if you smoked an entire garbage bag full. In spite of this fact hemp was included alongside marijuana as a Schedule I controlled substance in the Comprehensive Drug Abuse Prevention and Control Act of 1970. That same Schedule I listing is also home to lysergic acid diethylamide (LSD)and heroin.[2]

Speculation abounds as to why hemp was made illegal and who exactly was behind it. To a distracted public, Congress banned hemp because it was said to be a violent and dangerous drug. We would all benefit from a Truth Sculpture in that regard.

This is a case where sophists won and enacted a law that makes us all lose together.

Legalize Industrial Hemp. It is time the U.S. join other industrialized nations and stop demonizing hemp. The reality is hemp is an amazing resource to nearly every industry and product. This gift from nature has been cultivated for 12,000 years. It can provide humans with food, beverages, oils, fuel, paper, textiles, fabrics, plastics, and materials to build green housing including fiberboard, pressboard and hempcrete.[3] Hemp plants have been used for flood control and to fashion lightweight and strong automotive and aircraft parts. Hemp plants even clean up soil tainted with chemicals and radiation.[4]

Senator Ron Wyden (D-Oregon) has called for ending the federal ban on hemp production, "In my view, keeping the ban on growing hemp makes about as much sense as instituting a ban on portobello mushrooms. There's no reason to outlaw a product that's perfectly safe because of what it's related to."[5]

Truth Ticker. Politics is a filthy business where favors are exchanged that favor a few at the expense of many. Not all politicians are corrupt or lack integrity, but some are. People often vote against their own best interest, perhaps because they fall for the charmed smile that sociopaths can exude. The Truth Ticker exposes reality. Every appearance by a politician on television or in person is accompanied by a ticker (information feed) that shows who is supporting them, who they support, as well as whether what they are currently saying, is true.

With Truth Ticker you can see through political ads that smear opponents or distort issues. The Truth Ticker empowers people to separate fact from fiction. Egregious offenses will rightly earn a maxed out rating on the truth-lie-meter.

Mobile Truth Ticker. This is a smartphone app that allows the same functionality as you run your smartphone camera over the headlines and articles in a newspaper, magazine, or book in attempt to determine the truth.

See also: Truth Sculpture

Jury Sound Dome. Don't think of a pink elephant. Oh, too late. You've already thought of it. You can't *unthink* a thought. Likewise you can't *unhear* something you've just heard. And, you can't undo the connections and patterns that subsequently formed in your brain. Whatever you've heard is sure to influence your thoughts. That is precisely an instrument used by lawyers during trials to tamper with jurors' thoughts. They might knowingly expect an objection from the opposing lawyer or prosecutor and the judge may very well sustain the objection, but lawyers know once they plant the seed in the jurors' minds the effects are long lasting.

Our memories are not that easily purged. In light of this and given the absence of a commercially available Neuralyzer Memory Zapper, the juror box should be encased with a sound proof dome, the Jury Sound Dome[6] With the dome installed if the judge instructs the jury to disregard, then that will surely happen. Because of the time delay built into the audio, jurors will never hear what has been objected to. So when the judge says to the jury, "The jury will disregard," those jurors actually will have no other choice, but to disregard.

Bully Cream is intended for those people who have been bullied. It temporarily grants victims of bullying, the power of invisibility. As an agent of invisibility they are able to hide away and sulk or seek retribution. The widespread availability of this free cream will cause bullies to fear reprisal and cease their primitive behavior. In time, the pitiful practice of using ones strength to harm or intimidate those who are weaker will be a distant memory. Note: Bully Cream is not to be used for robbing banks.

Thief Go Blind. This immobilizer theft system temporarily renders blind, a thief attempting to burglarize a vehicle or premises. The blindness is alleviated by apology eye drops uniquely customized to the vehicle or premises. Apologizing to the victim and agreeing to restitution, and or other punishment would gain access to the eye drops.

Karmic Sensing Bullets need to be issued to all police forces, especially in the U.S. where "officer involved shooting" occurs too frequently. In the event an officer shoots his firearm at an innocent person, no matter the circumstances, Karmic Sensing Bullets would immediately drop to the ground upon leaving the firearm. Karmic

Sensing Bullets would, however, detect life threatening perpetrators and continue toward the target.

Social Justice. Whether it is conflicting parking signs that result in frequent parking tickets and impounds or "officer involved shootings" that result in dead citizens, let's surface it. Let's build a Truth Sculpture and then let's shame the injustice when we see it. If something is unfair, let's call it out and stamp it as such.

I think it is inhumane that metro bus drivers in the city of Seattle, and other cities for that matter, don't have adequate time or facilities to use the bathroom.[7] Adult diapers, clandestine coffee cans, and replacing urine-soaked driver seats are not desirable solutions.[8] We can do better.

But, we can also do better for the record levels of people experiencing homelessness. Again, in the city I call home, Seattle, this is a crisis.

Reframe. Often times, finding a solution to a persistent problem requires a Reframe. You need to look at the same old thing, but in a new way. Exploring innovative solutions doesn't follow established patterns.

A civically engaged populace often has fresh solutions or approaches that government insiders might not see. By inviting outsiders to the table, government can also free up the capacity of insiders and empower them to take risks and be more creative. People outside government inherently have more courage. After all, they don't fear losing the next election, or being fired. So, government should ask them for help.

Invite Citizens. Like Participatory Budgeting has shown us, people do like to be part of the solution. They especially appreciate this when they are able to propose fresh solutions as opposed to selecting from options proposed by politicians.

Intelligent informed citizens tire quickly of false choices that reflect anemic thinking on the part of politicians and policy makers. Inviting Citizens into an exploratory conversation might seem to waver from the full steam ahead approach to lock down one of the choices already on the table, but the ideation process is valuable. It increases civic engagement and can reveal solutions that were never on the table to begin with, possibly even the best solution.

Case in point. I am 99.9 percent certain that I have a solution that would work for any city that has the poopy bus driver problem. And, I'm confident my solution would be less expensive than solutions proposed by city/county/transit officials. My solution would not only solve the problem for bus drivers, it would demonstrate positive externalities for civic engagement, economic empowerment, and business development. My solution is something others would want to participate in, too.

So, aside from writing a book, how do you propose solutions to people who are running their version of the busy program? You could offer incentives, monetary or otherwise. Ah, you see, cities don't do that. It doesn't fit their pattern of behavior and expertise. We'll come back to that. First my solution....

Potty Decentral. Cities don't need to build more bathrooms. They need to gain access for bus drivers, to the built environment that already includes 1000's of bathrooms across coffee shops, restaurants, and businesses of all types. Incentives could be provided to those who provide access to their bathroom facilities, in order to offset the increased costs associated with water, soap, and paper.

The same access could be extended to people experiencing homelessness, or for that matter any person in the city. Imagine seeing the sign from participating businesses, "Bathrooms are always open here." Do you think that would send a positive and caring message that might spark repeat business from others? I do.

Everybody poops. It's so true that there is a children's book by that title. So, let's not pretend that bus drivers and those experiencing homelessness don't have to use the loo.

One potential byproduct of Potty Decentral would be that employment opportunities could be created for those experiencing homelessness. Bathrooms would be kept tidy and useable by some of the very people who would be using them.

See also: Mini Jobs

Notice that the Potty Decentral solution involves people rather than compelling or forcing them. Because the city and county have recently declared an emergency and public safety is at risk (both in the bus driver and homelessness situation) the government could compel selected businesses to participate using eminent domain.[9]

> "Seattle is facing an emergency as a result of the growing crisis in homelessness," said Mayor Murray. "The City is prepared to do more as the number of people in crisis continues to rise, but our federal and state partners must also do more. Cities cannot do this alone. Addressing homelessness must be a national priority with a federal response."[10]

Nobody likes to be compelled to do something. Eminent domain isn't necessary given the incentives and the sense of civic duty, if so invoked by a compelling campaign.

This is one citizen's view to one problem. Imagine all citizens everywhere, who have something to say about life in their city and how it could be better for those who work, live, recreate, or are simply passing through.

Now, this problem may pale in comparison to the refugee crisis faced by many government leaders. But, there is similar learning to be had. I'm skeptical that any government leader in any city has included refugees or citizens in designing solutions for refugees. It doesn't fit the normal pattern of authority dictating solutions and policy. If you know of a government leader in any city that has actually engaged in any form of voice of the customer analysis with refugees (or any marginalized population) please let me know.

Invented by People, Supported by Government. Imagine a campaign by that name, running across your city. Do you think it might inspire people to get involved or at least take a look? I think so.

Airbnb wasn't invented by a hotel brand. And, likewise the next solution to a government problem, such as homelessness, probably won't be invented by government. After all, government doesn't have a monopoly on all of the smart people and good ideas.

There have been a range of solutions to homelessness afforded by government and other organizations ranging from housing them to giving them bus tickets to leave town.[11]

Now, if you are from Switzerland or another democratic socialist country you might be reading this and thinking to yourself, "But, we don't have a homeless population." It's true, your citizens are probably more engaged and your government more representative of all people. You are more likely to have social safety nets and less likely to demonize the poor. You are more likely to oppose the things that cause people to become poor. You see issues as connected.

The chapters in this book were chosen, precisely because things are connected. You don't stem environmental degradation without addressing wealth and economy. And, it certainly doesn't live in a vacuum divorced of politics. So, let's start showing connections.

Data Observatory. The Data Science Institute resides on the Imperial College campus in South Kensington. It is currently home to over 50 researchers and collaborators with plans for expansion. Within the Data Science Institute is a data visualization studio and decision making space. The facility features an enveloping circular wall of 64 monitors powered by 32 computers facilitating 313 degrees of surround vision.[12] The idea of course is to make the sea of data that many organizations have been compiling, come to life.

Imagine access to such a system in for every city, large or small. Imagine collaboration between cities. In the county I live in there are 39 cities.

If we have overcrowded prisons, let's look at the data and the root causes. Are more people being shot by police or is that only media enflaming citizens. Let the data show the truth. Let's make it visible so that we can inform and possible change public policy. Similarly let's look at the history and data behind why bus drivers don't have a place to poop.

Before instituting new public policies lets run scenarios against the Data Observatory to see what positive and negative externalities surface.

The Data Observatory, the Internet and the sea of data that continues to amass, together enable what Buckminster Fuller dubbed as the World Game. That was an impossible idea at the time, but now it is quite possible. From the Buckminster Fuller Institute;

World Game. "In the 1960's Buckminster Fuller proposed a 'great logistics game' and 'world peace game' (later shortened to simply, the 'World Game') that was

190

intended to be a tool that would facilitate a comprehensive, anticipatory, design science approach to the problems of the world. The use of 'world' in the title obviously refers to Fuller's global perspective and his contention that we now need a systems approach that deals with the world as a whole, and not a piece meal approach that tackles our problems in what he called a 'local focus hocus pocus' manner.

Fuller chose to call his vision a 'game' because he wanted it seen as something that was accessible to everyone, not just the elite few in the power structure who thought they were running the show. In this sense, it was one of Fuller's more profoundly subversive visions.

Fuller wanted a tool that would be accessible to everyone, whose findings would be widely disseminated to the masses through a free press, and which would, through this ground-swell of public vetting and acceptance of solutions to society's problems, ultimately force the political process to move in the direction that the values, imagination and problem solving skills of those playing the democratically open world game dictated.

It was a view of the political process that some might think naive, if they only saw the world for what it was when Fuller was proposing his idea (the 1960s) — minus personal computers and the Internet.

The World Game that Fuller envisioned was to be a place where individuals or teams of people came and competed, or cooperated to: 'Make the world work, for 100% of humanity, in the shortest possible time, through spontaneous cooperation, without ecological offense or the disadvantage of anyone.'"[13]

Imagine the civic engagement if every resident of a city played the equivalent of the World Game.

Political Punch List. A punch list is usually a construction term used to indicate the final list of items to be completed before a contractor is paid. Each of us has a punch list of sorts. You might even have one for your household, combined family priorities, things to do, things to purchase, people to visit, places to go, appointments, home repairs, etc.

Neighborhoods have punch lists, too. That is the invisible list of issues, priorities, concerns, and the events scheduled for the neighborhood such as block parties, planned power outages, etc.

Politicians represent people who live in neighborhoods and communities. So, doesn't it make sense that they should know the priorities, ideas, concerns, etc. of the people? Of course it makes sense and this information should comprise the Political Punch List.

In the future, politicians are more connected to the people they serve. This can also help to surface spending priorities and inform public policy.

See also: Participatory Budgeting

Concerns and data from local government can roll up to county and state or provincial governments which in turn can help inform leaders and policy makers in the federal government. We are now shaping a schematic for a functional and informed public policy that represents the peoples' interests, not solely the lobbyists that frequent legislatures.

But, what about when there doesn't seem to be a government audience available, or one who cares about your delay, injustice, poor treatment, etc. That is when you need some impartial help.

Create an Ombudsman. The most interesting problems to solve and opportunities to explore, often happen at the edges and boundaries of any person's or department's purview. This is true in organizations of all types, including government.

Frustrated citizens, residents, and even employees might need help navigating government organizations. They might simply feel marginalized and wish to be heard or lodge a complaint. But, they may also have the best solution to a pressing problem. Or, they may surface a problem not yet on the radar of government agencies and officials.

The Ombudsman, can provide assistance identifying resources with whom to further engage and build momentum.

The Ombudsman is impartial and adheres to norms in all interactions with all audiences: complainants, public servants, elected representatives, stakeholders, community groups and members of the public across the community.

The Ombudsman doesn't have to solely be the chief complaint officer. They can also be chief champion of good ideas and promoter of progress, too. Ombudsmen are champions of social justice, fairness, access, and human rights. They are skilled in conflict resolution, effective and accessible service delivery, the advancement of human rights, and the promotion of accountability and responsiveness by government.

With an ombudsman available in every city, the future is indeed, brighter.

What About You?

The real world outside our laws and systems has an order to it. Truth and facts should reign supreme over the oratory craftsmanship of sophists and the subsequent draftsmanship by legislatures.

The ideas in this chapter, once implemented, represent an upgraded political operating system. This isn't an abandonment of democracy or government, or a cry for any specific ideology over another. It is simply what has been needed, better government, better citizens, and better tools and data to work smarter together.

If you ask a group of qualified, intelligence people if they would be interested in running for office, you are likely to hear a resounding NO. Good capable people are turned off by the current political system in droves. Me, too.

So what about you? In the future, as we upgrade the political operation system, you'll want to run for office. Serving others becomes meaningful again. If you don't run for office you'll at least want to be involved.

If you were in a boat that was taking water, you can either do something or do nothing. Well, planet earth has been taking on water. You decide how you will act. Recall Martin Niemöller's poem, "First they came...." At what point do you decide to do something different, no matter how small, or grandiose. The world needs you. But, you're also needed somewhere else.

11 FAMILY & PETS

Home is where the heart is. You feel good traveling and visiting others, but unless you suffer from perpetual wanderlust at some point you long to be home with family and friends. Home often includes pets. Even those who don't have pets relish in the pets they've had or those of others. If pets cleaned up after themselves, more people would have them. Also, when our pets disappear on us for hours or days on end, we worry. But, domesticated animals also miss their caretakers, or more accurately from the perspective of the animal — the one who gives them food.

Come Home Collar. Let Fido or Snowball know it is time to come home by sending a message directly to their collar. The collar releases a comforting smell or sound that your pet associates with home, you, and possibly feeding time. On command, or on a predetermined schedule, your Come Home Collar-trained companion is ready to follow your signal.

Doo Gone is the ultimate dog doo disposer. No more

plastic bags and picking up that steaming, smelly, mushy, mess. Best of all, there is no need to carry it away. The two part solution turns your canine's mess into harmless sand. First, sprinkle the key lime crystals over the droppings and then spritz with the sand-it spray. Voila, in a few moments your canine's mess turn into harmless, odorless sand. Leave it in place or spread it with your foot. "What? No! My dog didn't do anything here."

Rose Rump Composter. Attach this device to the rear of your dog and no longer stoop to pick up dog poop. With the Rose Rump Composter your canine is self contained. When you return from your walk or trip to the dog park, simply detach from your dog and spread the composting pellets in your garden or the landscape.

Use the gargantuan size for your horse. Carriage passengers no longer smell wafts of manure as the composter emits a fragrant rose smell.

Snail Eating Mechanical Rodent. This pet and people friendly robot patrols sidewalks and parking lots for snails. Appearing like a robotic armadillo once it finds a snail it slurps it up, like a dust bunny to a vacuum cleaner. The robot is maintenance free and recognizes faces and language. Out walking on your sidewalk you might encounter one of these polite robots talking to you, "Hello Mrs. Olson. How are you? Very good then, I've got to get back to work." Moments later … "Hello Mr. Snail. Slurp!"

Good news — the Snail Eating Mechanical Rodent, like a regular rodent, will eat dog doo as well. Empty it like the Rose Rump Composter to create garden pellets.

Bird View Channel. We are more empathetic when we see the view from the perspective of others, whether they are bees, birds, or other people. Imagine picking out a bird or cat or any animal in the natural landscape and then pressing the "view" button on your smartphone. Then the view from the perspective of the animal appears on your screen for you to see what they see. Get to know your pets and visiting animals in your neighborhood. Know what it is like to fly over that tree, hover while collecting nectar, or hide under the porch spying on humans.

Bird Translator. Use the bird translator to eavesdrop on bird conversations. It translates bird communications into human understandable language. Talk back to the bird, too. Bird Translator will convert your human words into bird understandable language.

Depress Detect. Everybody has a family member near or far that has suffered from the invisible disability of depression. Perhaps you are one. But, do you even know? Depress Detect is the early warning system that detects when a person is feeling off their game. Feeling off your game isn't bad by itself, it is the downward spiral of depression that can follow. So, Depress Detect looks for the little things that reveal your mood, those things that may be in your blind spot, but that sensitive pets or trained machines could detect.[1][2] Tone, temperature, facial expression, and even gait can reveal signs of depression.

Depress Detect's sensory prowess and communications network is an integrated system that works across your clothing and shoes, home furnishings and devices you interact with. Imagine a Depress Detect equipped mirror that you gaze into each morning, reading your facial expressions and adding it to your profile. Then throughout the rest of the day as you talk on the phone, type on your keyboard, and even walk, the system continues to watch over you like a nurturing mother. This isn't a creepy dragnet of mass surveillance that the NSA was exposed for by Edward Snowden. This is human-centric health information that helps each us to be the healthiest person we can be, leading to better families and communities.

The system will suggest actions you can take or even foods to consume that could improve your condition. But, in the event the person so afflicted isn't paying attention or upon reaching a level of concern, it will notify family and friends. Depress Detect provides alerts to check in, nurture, counsel, listen, and maybe even just provide a hug or encouragement.

The key is to break the cycle of isolation and despair that accompanies depression that left unchecked, could result in major depression. At that point, it is physically impossible for a person to "snap out of it"; a person will need medication to restore the chemical pathways that are no longer functioning correctly in their brains.

Depress detect might have the unintended consequence of putting depression treatment drugs in the museum, but that's okay because along with it, it may sunset the suicide that, sadly, sometimes accompanies major depression. Rest in peace dear Robin Williams, Dale L. and the many others so afflicted that they decided to prematurely leave this life and their families behind.

Okay, that subject was a little depressing. Now let's look at some impossible ideas that are more lighthearted.

Baby Stick is a harmless spray that temporarily immobilizes your baby. Freeze your baby safely in place wherever it's at, on the couch, on the floor, in the airport, etc. Babies stick without incident and without the need to watch over them. Mom and dad can tend to that interruption or emergency without putting baby in harm's way.

Baby Talker translates your child's screams, cries, pouts, and other noises into intelligible language that moms and dads can understand. Take the guess work out of comforting your child. The medical talk feature provides a diagnosis for conditions that may require medical attention.

Snot Dissolve is a wand that you run over your child's schnozzle. Watch their mucus disappear. It frees them to breath more easily. They'll think you're a hero. Might as well call this idea "hero maker."

Baby Silence is a noise canceling ear bud system. Moms who love the cry of a colicky baby can still tune in to their noisy baby station. But, for the rest of us, we'd rather do without. Whether on the plane or in the car or at a restaurant — silence is golden.

The related in-flight feature turns a restless kid's legs to the equivalent of rubber. No more feeling the back of your airplane seat being kicked.

The Open Handset Alliance is the group of companies that collaborated to bring the world Android, the operating system that now dominates over 80 percent of mobile devices.

In their quest to build a better phone, they looked partly to children. Early on, the Open Handset Alliance talked to kids and asked them to tell what their dream phone would do. They captured the children's response in a video, "If I had a magic phone."[3] We could all learn from that experience.

> **"Grown men can learn from very little children,**
> **for the hearts of the little children are pure,**
> **and therefore, the Great Spirit may show to them**
> **many things which older people miss."**

Black Elk
Medicine Man, Warrior,
Priest, Holy Man, Heyoka
Sioux Indians
(1863–1950)

Child Speaks. If we are to have great families, in great neighborhoods, in great communities then we'll have to care about what children think and how they feel.

Hierarchy doesn't matter. Remember might does not make right, not in the business world and not in the neighborhood. Everything is contextual. The kid selling lemonade is the leader for the day, bringing delight to others. Take off your parent-hat and listen to kids in another way.

Don't be afraid of the unknown and unproven and above all don't fear failure. It will be fine. Develop and cultivate talent, provide opportunity, let the kids mow the lawn, let them help plan the next family outing. Let kids lead projects they would otherwise not think to lead. Create involvement and build community. What else could we be asking children?

o   What do you think about?
o   What do you know about?
o   Who would you help if you could?
o   How would you help them?
o   How do you feel?
o   What would you want to do?
o   What is your opinion on … ?
o   Do you want to get involved with … ?
o   What do you want to learn?

When we ask kids these questions, we build their awareness of issues and increase their empathy for others. When we get them to talk about their feelings in a constructive way we have emotionally healthy children. If you were to hear, "That's not fair," then it's time to build a Truth Sculpture.

Now imagine all of those questions on a Child Speaks platform that is kid-centric, driven by kids, that invites parents, teachers, and the community to join. This will create kids who are more interested and interesting. It will also create healthier and more productive relationships between all parties. Oh, the possibilities.

Dream Screen. I'm going to tell you a story about a duck. I recently had a dream about a giant duckling. It was a strange dream, like many dreams are. I was in a garden or maybe it was a farm. Baby ducks were being born, more like simply appearing. The ducks were born with two parts. The tiny head and the diminutive body with it fragile bat-like wings, connected by a tiny string sized neck.

One duck in particular was born with its head completely separated from its lifeless body. It wasn't clear in my dream why this happened. The duckling seemed to simply appear; there were no shells to poke through and emerge from. It's a dream, please forgive the nonsensical nature.

Sadly, I placed this lifeless duckling in, from best I can recall, a birdbath looking compost bin. The bin was more like a birdbath, but deeper and contained organic material as well as liquid. I went about my business in the garden and at one point I looked over to witness one eye on the half submerged duckling slightly open, looking in my direction.

Somehow the little duckling had connected its head to its body and it began to show signs of life. I was afraid the liquid in the compost ooze would somehow decompose the duckling if I didn't rescue it. I spooned the tiny creature out, rinsed it with cold water to free it of the compost muck. Then I ran warm water over it to arouse its inner workings. The duckling responded favorably. Both eyes opened, it began to move on its own, and within minutes it could move its wings and walk about on its own.

Over the next few days I noticed this duckling was standing out from the others that had recently appeared. When I observed the ducking waddling across the grass, this previously lame duck, was now stronger, taller, and more resilient than the others. It literally towered above the other ducklings, about five times their height. Hence the name of my dream is Giant Duckling.

Now, I've tried to recall this story best I could. But, it suffers two faults. First, I may have imperfect recall of my dream, perhaps even misremembering certain nuances. And, the other fault is that I'm unable to fully express in words what I saw and the experience that I had. For these reasons I'd like to see an impossipreneur create the Dream Screen. Because if you liked the Giant Duckling story in words, I think that you'd like it even better on the screen.

You would benefit from Dream Screen, too. When you find yourself unable to find the words that fully describe your dream you can rely on Dream Screen. Simply replay the recorded dream to share with others. They are then able to view it like any other movie. Remember before you begin playback of your masterpiece, you might want to start with the disclaimer, "Okay now, remember when you watch this, it's only a dream."

Moms and dads can now peer into their kids' dreams or nightmares and better understand and provide comfort to their children. Without relying on words, dream screen will even work for toddlers who have yet to fully develop language skills. Now imagine what those dreams would look like on the screen.

Dream screen would also be useful in the understanding and treatment of people with disorders of the mind and those suffering from post-traumatic stress disorder (PTSD).

We love our pets and family. But, sometimes we can encounter conflict that tests that love. Some of these are bathroom related.

Smarty Toilet. This gender sensing toilet with facial recognition automatically raises and lowers the toilet seat, according to the gender and bathroom business about to be done, e.g., is it boomaloom or beemaleem? While you doing your business, the companion sink warms enough water for you to wash your hands. The toilet automatically flushes for you and gently reminds you to please wash your hands.

Smarty Sink. The companion to Smarty Toilet, this sink has a predetermined allotment of warm water. Smarty Sink flashes a gentle green light to indicate when it's ready for you to place your soapy hands under the faucet. Voila — warm local water.

Smarty Sink automatically reclaims the soapy water used to wash your hands. This water become available to the Smarty Toilet for the next flush. Using Smarty Toilet and Smarty Sink preserves freshwater resources and eliminates the spread of germs, including E. coli, which makes people sick.

Sampling Commode. People can and will be fooled, but it is much harder to fool sensors. Every human being eventually empties their bladder and evacuates their bowel; a fact that plays out over the course of our lives.

Bowel movements can provide valuable health information. Stools can be tested for certain types of bacteria, parasites, or viruses. Testing can also reveal digestive problems such as the malabsorption of certain sugars, fats, or nutrients.[4]

The Sampling Commode senses human waste before sending it on to the sewer system. Not only can the Sampling Commode alert you if someone in your household has a health problem it can also detect drug use. Now the concerned parent who gets little response to the question, "How was school today?" can at least put their mind to rest that their child isn't taking drugs. The Sampling Commode can reveal drug use early on, before it becomes a habit. It can also be your ally in the early detection of health problems.

Odor Defender. Smack down odors with this flatulence containment system. This personal protection companion device and smartphone application provides an early warning system alerting the user to offending odors nearby. "WARNING: dirty diaper smell at six o'clock low."

In the event of direct contact, a fragrant deodorizer or ion generator will automatically discharge in the direction of the assailant. Furniture of the future contains Odor Defender technology to make guests more comfortable. It also preserves the lives of couches and chairs that may otherwise be discarded prematurely.

The Neighborhood

For most people life is better shared with family and pets. Households are like little neighborhoods — best when people understand one another, get along, and there is no conflict.

The ideas in this chapter help to do just that, namely detect and prevent trouble, increase our understanding of one another, reduce potential conflict, and create dialogue about things that matter. We need this in order to thrive at home and in the larger neighborhood.

But, we also want to thrive outside the home. So, in the next chapter we'll explore an area where we spend enormous amount of time, over the course of our lives.

"A good community will not be invented, discovered or 'just grow.' It must be forged from the purpose and quality of the lives of the people living in it."

Arthur Ernest Morgan
Community Organizer, Educator,
Civil Engineer, U.S. Administrator
(1878–1975)

12 THE WORLD OF WORK

In the future life is more about living. It isn't so much about trading hours for dollars or Euros. That doesn't mean that work doesn't get done. There is plenty of work to be done. What it means is that our mindset becomes about completing projects, pursing initiatives, creating the new, and improving the old. With a more thoughtful society and the social safety net that goes along with it, there is more collaboration, flatter pay between the top and the bottom of an organization, and poverty gets put in the museum. All people have the ability to contribute to society. A more evolved society doesn't tolerate trillions of dollars sitting idle or the making of billionaires, while others die in abject poverty. No, we are the dominant species on the planet. As such, we will eventually make a shift from producing killing machines and from creating policies that divide us, and instead move toward creating a more tolerant society who embraces diversity and is obsessed with making life more peaceful and worth living.

A National Goal. Happiness is a good metric for people in any society. Full employment for those who want it should be a national goal and priority. The ability to make meaning and provide for oneself and family goes a long way toward making people happy. This is the surest way to strengthen communities, build healthy innovation neighborhoods, and advance human progress. In the future, research and polling organizations like Gallup.com will work with all individuals on a fully inclusive basis to measure their happiness across a range of factors. Politicians will be held to account for the happiness of the people they govern.

Full Engagement. In the past, the majority of employees were not engaged at work. Still others were actively disengaged.[1] Just as happiness is a good national goal it is also a good goal to have within the workplace. Full Engagement matches the talent and interest of employees to assignments that they would likely excel at. Trained professionals from the Make Meaning Department are available to help. With the Innovation Clearinghouse, there are many more assignments that transcend for-profit, nonprofit, and government organizations. With the boundaries less rigid between organizations, employees are exposed to more diversity, can increase their skills, build their support networks, and become more engaged at work, and in the community.

Innovation Neighborhood. Great potential exists for established large businesses that already have products, services, distribution channels, customers, and infrastructure. Creating an Innovation Neighborhood builds on that momentum. Adding outside entrepreneurs to the Innovation Neighborhood adds fractional talent that organizations might not otherwise attract for a job. Many talented people want to work with an organization, but not necessarily for that same organization; the Innovation Neighborhood builds a bridge between them.

Mini Jobs. Modeled after the mini-jobs in Germany,

Mini Jobs enable employers to add talent to their organization with minimal paperwork and hassle. The same is true for the talent. There are no employment taxes paid by either party. These Mini Jobs are intended to provide supplemental income to those who need it. Mini Jobs could be used by employers to run experiments. It is likely and expected that many of these jobs will turn into full time jobs as those experiments pay off.

See also: Make Meaning Department, Universal Basic Income, and Future Coworking Spaces

Nobody likes to feel stuck, whether they are working on their own, alongside a team, or not working at all. Getting help when and where it's needed can fuel human progress and help you reach your potential.

Need Detect. One of the shortcoming of the human mind is that we seldom learn from those who came before. If you wish to become an astronaut it pays to talk to current astronauts and those of the past. But, too often we think our own circumstances to be so unique that we couldn't possibly learn from others.

Right now on any subject there is a person about to make a mistake that somebody else has already learned from. Need Detect capitalizes on that frequent occurrence. When you are stuck and want a clear path forward, it is time to have a discussion with Need Detect. The artificially intelligent interviewer assembles data and scenarios that match your line of inquiry. If at any point you wish to speak with a human operator, you may do so. The purpose is to unstick your mind and free you to continue making progress on your journey no matter the subject, unless of course it harms humanity or the environment, then you are on your own.

See also: Lifeline

Robot Surrogate. Robots will increasingly displace workers, whether the replacements appear as a movie kiosk, an automated welder, robotic flight attendant, driverless truck, etc. Few people are immune from this reality.

Robots can help boost productivity, but they don't help the people they displace or the communities that become starved of tax revenue.

In spite of this, in the future, the robot could be doing us all a favor, but only if we take precautions. A tax on automation can contribute to our collective progress. Here is how. Part of the tax goes toward retraining the person displaced. That portion of the tax is retired when the person is once again gainfully employed. The tax also funds city, state, and federal government to invest in further progress. This creates progress for all people not just robot owners or those who manufacture them.

> **"Work keeps at bay**
> **three great evils:**
> **boredom, vice, and need."**
>
> *pen name, Voltaire*
> *Francois-Marie Arouet*
> *Writer, Historian,*
> *Philosopher Polemicist*
> *(1694–1778)*

Morale Bot. When the boss is behaving badly it usually affects many people. When that happens, Morale Bot is needed. Morale Bot is part internal affairs investigator and part robot. When the robot has heard enough complaints from employees or contractors it takes the boss by the hands and escorts them out of the building. They are not fired or flogged at this point, they are merely taken on a walk. Hand in hand they walk with the Morale Bot. To regain entry they have to discuss with the robot, their bad behavior. Eventually they have to overcome the robot's skepticism meter that is built to protect the teams' interests.

Visual Issue Reporter. Often time when you are working with a team progress can become halted. Most of the time it isn't apparent why. The Visual Issue Reporter monitors a team's progress towards it goals. It can reveal to groups the relative alignment of team members on various issues. This is important because the members themselves are often unable to articulate what is going on.

Regeneration Station. One of the benefits people have in working from home is that if they need a little recharge, they can take a nap, or lay down on the floor to stretch out. Too many workplaces don't have adequate spaces to disconnect momentarily from the cubicle or office environment. A Regeneration Station provides employees with napping cots and pillows for personal regeneration. The Regeneration Station could be a shared resource among companies that share the same physical location.

Job Declare. Imagine your peaceful travel was interrupted mid-flight with the announcement over the intercom, is there a doctor on board the aircraft? During a medical emergency you're very likely to hear the flight attendant ask this question. If life, sometimes you know what you need. That used to be nearly always the case, because the world was less specialized. Now, most job titles and duties are utterly unintelligible to people outside those occupations.

So, for many industries and situations, the likelihood that somebody will ask the equivalent of "Is there a doctor?" is remote.

Often times there is a performance gap between the organization's current state and their potential. This can make for some terrible suffering among customers, patients, visitors, guests, or whatever types of audiences a particular organization serves. But, it can also make for some terrible performance for investors. It can even ruin a company entirely.

Job Declare allows knowledgeable individuals to declare a job after seeing a need they can fill. The job can be a temporary assignment or one that become a permanent part of the organization. It's okay if the position goes away, because in the future we have a safety net, Universal Basic Income, a Make Meaning Department, and Innovation Clearinghouse, that are always looking for people to help advance human progress. What job will you declare? For me, I'll start with designing better experiences and services at my local cable monopoly.

Humans Served First

In the future, whether you have a J-O-B where you regularly report for duty in exchange for a paycheck, or you piece together assignments and get paid periodically, you will benefit from the ideas presented in this chapter.

Most likely throughout your life you'll bounce between periods of stability to those less certain.

This was a problem in the past. Depending upon which country you live in, there may be little safety net. At the same time, those who may have sidelined your talent may be doing fabulously well.

In the future, global citizens are less tolerant of this sort of behavior that plunders people and the planet.

The future of work looks bright. It is more participatory, it is more impactful, and it better aligns to our individual needs and interests. Our talents can be recognized, put to use, and further cultivated.

All of us, working together, for the benefit of all. We can put a stop to those things that don't put humans first.

In the next chapter, we'll explore the intersection of computers and communications, two devices that sometimes forget to put humans first.

13 COMPUNICATIONS

This could be called technology, but technology also resides in all of the other categories. So, this category captures the specific idea behind what most of us are thinking about in terms of technology that doesn't have a specialized purpose. So we have computers and communications. It is the blurring of the two words.

What is This? - Visual Search Engine. You see a flower while out walking. You take a photo and send it to search. The What is This? - Visual Search Engine tells you what you are viewing even when you don't know the words. This is different than image search engines that require you enter the words that describe the image you are looking for. It also differs from image search sites that merely tell you where your uploaded image can be found on the Web. When you can see something plainly in front of you but don't know what it is, it is time for a What is This? - Visual Search Engine. This is also useful when you are in another country and don't understand the local language.

Hacker Smacker. This defensive firewall device acts as

a boomerang. When hacking activity is detected the hacker smacker first safeguards the intended victims computing device and then seeks out the perpetrator, eventually crashing their storage drive. This will put an end to the notices from governments, insurance companies, past employers, retailers, and others that your personal information may have been compromised.

Biometric Leash. This wrist leash is a biometric device that makes your computer or phone only accessible to you while you are wearing your leash. It creates a 1:1 connection between you and your computer. Nobody else can mimic your leash. It is unique to you, because you are a unique biological snowflake.

In the future, when you make a call to a company or government agency they don't require you to re-authenticate. Voice and computer communications authenticate you through your biometric leash.

In the future, stolen credit cards and personal information will not be valuable. Systems will increasingly require truly unique and secure credentials and that will come from the Biometric Leash. There will be no secondary market for stolen information and devices, except as recycled components.

Instant On. In the future computers and communication devices catch up to people. They turn on when you want them on. They are accessible immediately. The archaic term "boot time" is history, no longer relevant. There are also no programs that compete for attention at startup as if they are saying, "Pick me, pick me."

Compute Restore. In the event a computing device crashes in the future, it is returned to its precise pre-crash status with all programs and services intact.

No longer do computer users have to remember what

they had open, which versions of saved programs, which emails they had culled from their inbox, etc.

Visual Email. In the future email becomes more structured and visual, so when it is connected to other emails you see it. You can rearrange and group emails according to your own criteria.

My Journeys service is human-centric software that captures your interactions and stores relevant data on your behalf. Traditionally when a person interacts with a government agency or with a company those interactions are stored in some type of software system, usually Customer Relationship Management software. But, sadly, even though customer is in the title of the software category (CRM), the customer doesn't have access or a view to their own data. Accessing and viewing data remains the privilege of the company or agency you're interacting with.

In our own lives we have many journeys as we deal with agencies and companies over time. The My Journey software application interacts with all of them, but puts the data into the hands of customers. Now you have all of the recorded interactions, contact information, contracts you've agreed to and the separation date, history, scheduled service dates, etc. When you fire the company and move on to another brand, you retain your data. Finally, it is "about you."

Smart Software Learns. Too many times technology companies design products that are well imagined, but fall short on usability. Smart Software Learns from user behavior and then modifies the user interface and features to suit a user's particular workflow. When computers and the software that powers them adapt to fit the workflow of users, then computers have finally become user friendly.

Treating users as though they were like the people who

built the software is wrong. So is pushing a common product configuration to users irrespective of whether they are expert or novice.

Eye Mouse Move. Many people, myself included, use dual monitors and wear glasses. When "in the zone" people are using the keyboard quickly and dread having to slow down by having to use the mouse. Imagine being able to direct the mouse cursor to a location on either monitor simply by having your eyes linger in an area coordinated with a blink. The sensor to detect this eye movement could be easily affixed to ordinary eyewear.

Digital Paperbook. This hybrid book gives you the feel of paper pages you can actually write on combined with the benefits of digital books. You can flip through pages, skim content, and read anywhere, even with no power. But, the Digital Paperbook provides you with useful digital features, too. Bookmarks, highlighting, and search features combined with note-taking and device memory help the reader to navigate, learn, and return to the last page read.

Embedded functionality in the paper provides the intelligence and the communication links to your companion screen. Now you can actually work across mediums. You no longer have to make a false choice between the print or digital versions.

Digital Paperbook also applies to newspapers and magazines. This could be the rebirth of the newspaper industry. The larger format and professional layout of newspapers is desirable. But, without a bridge to a digital world the paper versions become disconnected relics. So, let's combine the two.

Linky Newspapers give the reader the ability to finger select a link and then play a video or sound file on a companion device. The reader can also store and forward for retrieval later. There isn't any need to rekey the information into your computer or smartphone. Linky Newspapers value the readers time and provide them with an experience worthy of remarking on.

Beacon Enabled Maps give users the luxury of a large foldable paper map with the added features normally reserved for GPS and wayfinding applications. Imagine while walking around in a city you could roll out a map and actually see your current location, blinking on it. Highlight your destination and track yourself along your route without having to rely on a tiny screen or even the need for a cell phone. Pick up a Beacon Enabled Map wherever you travel.

Parking Minder alert is a service to drivers that reveals the hazards of parking in specific locations. It examines previous parking and impound data for each GPS location and resolves the signs that govern that exact parking location. This eliminates parking tickets and impounds that drivers experience due to conflicting or confusing parking signs. This leads to a better city experience for residents and travelers alike.

In the future cities will have to find sources of revenue elsewhere and perhaps repurpose or retire judges who previously made their living through aggressive enforcement of bad public policy.

Sorry cities you'll have to find other ways to make up the shortfall. It will no longer be coming from the drivers who work, live, recreate, or pass through the city you govern.

Of course if driver use the self driving options of Chapter 6 they'll never need to worry about parking at all.

Direct-to-Author Technology is beneficial to readers and writers alike. While reading a book, readers are able to capture their sentiment or comments in context and then share with the author or others in the community. Better than social media alone, Direct-to-Author technology provides context, the very page or words or image you wish to comment on. Easily spark a conversation with the author or between readers.

Reader Aware Books. Automatically track emotions as you read a book, then share how it made you feel. Reader Aware Books sense changes in pupil, pulse and temperature. A Reader Aware Book could even adjust itself as you read, either rewriting itself offering up alternative threads in the story or even compiling a personal dictionary of words you stumble over.

Finger Swipe and Store. Gliding your finger across a touch smartphone gives you the option to copy data to the clipboard. In the past, sharing that data required that you paste it to another application on the same device or send the data directly using the capabilities of the phone. Practically speaking, this means you had to email, text, or otherwise share the data in the cloud, even though the sending and receiving devices might be next to each other. It also required that you know the email address or phone number. Imagine a different scenario.

Finger Swipe and Store give you local storage capability. on a finger peripheral that you can use to capture or deposit data. Perhaps you wish to pick up data from something you are reading. Finger Swipe and Store accommodates the digital and analog world. If you can swipe it, you can store it. This means you can continue watching a video in your driverless car or any publicly available screen that you were originally watching at home or work. Finger swipe the video before you leave and then swipe to deposit elsewhere. Not finished listening to the podcast before you have to leave? No problem, finger swipe it and then deposit it onto your radio playback device as you enter a vehicle.

Data is picked up and stored on your finger can be shared with any other device including remote controls, touch screens, computer peripherals, public screens, audio systems, or even other finger storage devices.

Crowpass. This is a password replacement scheme that uses your biometric data that is largely unchanged over time. Crows never forget a face. And, your own body doesn't forget you, so why should your computer, phone, applications and other services? You can't fake a unique you, not to crows and not to future applications, services, and devices. Crowpass is secure and convenient and works in cooperation with the Biometric Leash.

Go Faster Button. Some things take way too long, like autosave on the computer. Worse yet, most companies that make products don't understand how horrible of an experience this is for the user. The Go Faster Button makes you the priority and puts you to the front of the line, not the program or service that has temporarily taken over your phone or computer.

When the user invokes the Go Faster Button it captures the data and context and shares it with the offending organization so they can make improvements. It also automatically updates the public record that will later be used to shame the organization(s) if there are no improvements or remedies. Part of that public record is the time cumulatively wasted by people that could otherwise be living life.

A colleague of mine plays the harmonica during his computer's lengthy boot-up time as a way to cope with the uncontrollable situation.

Stop Now Button. If you were to accidentally turn on the wrong light in your home, you could immediately recover. You would simply turn it off and the light would immediately respond.

But, if you were to click the wrong icon or link on the computer you have no recourse but to wait for the computer to finish its sequence of instructions and services. Your human brain may have immediately detected the mistake, but you are left waiting for the computer to catch up to you, if it ever does.

The Stop Now Button returns the power to humans. Technology is there to serve us, not the other way around. When a user invokes the Stop Now Button, it really does interrupt the path last taken, returning the computer to a usable and desirable state.

A New Enlightenment

Computers and communication devices have come a long way. It's hard to imagine life without them. Though the real world is still an analog world, the digital world has encroached nearly every aspect of our lives. And, that is not a bad thing.

Humans are superior (at least so far) at recognizing patterns, adapting to changing situations, and working with and without a script. But, computers are excellent at other things including following instructions and working with large amounts of data. They should be used to compliment humans' imperfect memory, inability to conceive large numbers, and the inability to perform computations quickly and reliably.

By leveraging the strengths of both, computing devices and humans can accomplish much more together.

Most of the ideas in this chapter exist because we haven't yet exerted that leverage. Though humans are imperfect they can immediately recognize the shortcomings of technology. Too often, devices and services fail to delight and sometimes to even satisfy.

But, among these same imperfect humans, are the

designers, engineers, and entrepreneurs whose own impatience and intolerance for poor design will continue to push computing and communications forward. Ironically, as they do, those very devices they create will further emulate their inferior human masters.

14 SUPERPOWERS

Abook on impossipreneurs would not be complete without superpowers. Inspired by cartoons, science fiction, and our own imaginations we've all imagined having powers beyond the reach of ordinary humans.

Invisibility is the ability to become undetected by others. Even better than being invisible to the naked human eye is to become invisible to all emissions, sound, thermal and otherwise. If you possessed this superpower you might have people with the next superpower wondering where those thoughts are coming from.

Telepathy is the communication of thoughts or ideas by means other than the known senses.

Thought Broadcaster is a smartphone application that enables its users to point their phone at a target mind, press the read thoughts button and then enjoy (or be terrified) of the continuous stream of thoughts channeled directly from the targeted mind. Thoughts appear on the smartphone display and are optionally heard over the phone's speaker in speakerphone mode, or privately with earbuds.

Object Pass allows you to bend your atoms around objects so you appear to bounce or pass through them. With this superpower you'll never stub your toe again. You'll also not suffer any other attack or physical danger. Object Pass allows you to simply bend around or pass through, but never feel a collision or interfere with another object. This is a very useful superpower for clumsy people who bump into things or those whose inner person was placed in too large of a body. Object Pass is also known as Accident Prone be Gone.

Arm Extend or the power of elasticity gives you instant access to an extended flexible arm. Now you'll never lose that glass about to fall off the counter. You can pick up objects normally out of reach, those on the top shelf, or atop the cupboard, or even on the roof. Other practical uses for this superpower include rescuing a cat out of a tree, scratching the middle of your back, or reaching into the back seat. And perhaps most practically, while walking in crowds bewilder strangers with the classic game of *Did somebody just tap me on my shoulder?*

Temporal Rewind is the ability to rewind time. Once you've rewound time you can make a better decision, have the opportunity for a redo, stave off something terrible from happening, or simply relish a moment over and over again.

Manipulate Time. While you rewind you might as well summon your related superpower Manipulate Time so you can pass through time normally while you reduce the speed of everything surrounding you.

Eidetic Zoom Vision is the ultra-high resolution digital recorder that you always have with you. It is part recorder and part lenses — either implanted in or covering your eyes like contact lenses. Everything you look at is recorded.

With Eidetic Zoom Vision you can go back and retrace your steps. See what you may not have paid attention to at the time. Don't remember where you left your keys? No problem at all. Walk through your own experience as it unfolded.

Eidetic Zoom Vision is better than mere photographic memory because of the zoom capabilities. When you need more detail you can zoom in. Because Eidetic Zoom Vision records in ultra-high resolution, you are able to zoom in to view detail that either wasn't important at the time, or that you simply didn't pay attention to before.

Memory Search. You dreamt it. You saw it. You read it. It's right on the tip of your tongue or is it brain? But, now for whatever reason you cannot recall it. You are certain it's stored there somewhere in your brain. If only you could access it. You walked to the refrigerator, but now you can't remember why. Or, you see somebody you know, but don't remember how you know them. Memory search enables you to search your mental filing cabinet and retrieve whatever content you have stored there.

Bank-a-Thought is the superpower that enables you to bank a thought before it is inadvertently erased, or purged by other thoughts and actions. Bank-a-Thought allows you to store a thought at the moment it occurs, for later recall. I thought of this idea at 3:12 a.m. on a Tuesday. I didn't want to get out of bed. I wanted this superpower. But, too many dreams and ideas fade before fully waking and I didn't want that to happen, so this idea appears here. Obviously, I woke up enough to write down these ideas on a pad of paper. But, Bank-a-Thought would have been much more convenient.

Ideas often come at the most inconvenient times and circumstances such as: when driving, showering, snuggling with your loved one, or while enjoying a book. Because you don't have Bank-a-Thought, I've provided you with spaces to capture ideas throughout this book. I won't be offended if the ideas have no relationship whatsoever to this book. Our minds are funny that way. Oh, I just remembered I have a half a sandwich in the refrigerator.

Insta-Appear is the ultimate travelers superpower. Have you ever forgotten something at home while traveling? If you are like most people the answer is, of course. With Insta-Appear, whatever you've forgotten — toothbrush, hairspray, comb, passport, etc. — suddenly appears by your command. Ah, imagine how much lighter you can travel. Getting through security at the airport just got easier. Best of all, it isn't limited to travel. Insta-Appear is your faithful companion wherever you are.

Protective Bubble shields you from the rain, snow, or other elements. It will even protect you from sandstorms and fire. This is our personal shield. In hurricane mode it simply diverts the weather around you. Even tornadoes spin directly around you leaving you completely unharmed. The Protective Bubble can also be used to protect you from air born viruses, air pollution, and hurtful language directed at you.

Snap Mob. It is a well known phenomena that in crowds the level of morality is lowered and personal responsibility is lost. People in large crowds lose inhibitions and feel safe amid others behaving like them. They do things they would otherwise not do if acting alone, even engaging in violence. When they feel their behavior cannot be traced back to them, they are more likely to break social norms.[1] Mob mentality is dangerous for all involved. Snap Mob is a form of mind control that restores the individuality with each person exhibiting mob mentality. If police had this superpower they would never have to deal with riots. If rioters had this superpower they would not have to deal with police brutality. And, if potential victims had this power they would stop mob mentality before it fully blossomed.

A More Powerful You

Possessing superpower would be nice. Who wouldn't like to levitate an object or walk around undetected. Most of all, we'd be free from the rigors of an ordinary life and its attendant responsibilities. Imagining having superpowers gives us escape. It's like taking a nap and having a great dream, except the dream happens in real life while we are awake. How exciting; just imagine.

But, we needn't be super human to have super powers. Human strengths are powerful, too. The power to make someone smile or laugh isn't usually on the superpowers-to-acquire list. Because we all have this power already, doesn't make it less powerful.

Each of us also has the power to be resilient, learn, change our minds, and adapt. Hopefully, in reading this book, you are gaining a sense that you are more powerful than what you previously considered.

A powerful person like you can accomplish much. You can increase your empathy, make meaning, and help others to do the same. You can more intentionally evolve your relationships and become a better caretaker for your life and a better steward for the planet.

You can contribute to the propaganda for good network and help others to be on the right side of history. If you think about it, you don't really need superpowers, because you are already well equipped.

A good global citizen like you can accomplish much, in

your tiny corner of the world, and across the world. Have you ever wondered what point is exactly opposite you on the earth, your antipode? The antipode of your place on Earth is the point on the Earth's surface diametrically opposite you. Two points that are antipodal to each other are connected by a straight line running through the center of the Earth. Your antipode is also the point furthest from you if you were to travel around the earth's surface.

Use one of the free tools to find your antipode.[2] Then use social media and your network to make a new friend there.

If you are like me, and you find water opposite you, then pick the nearest land mass. Use the power you already possess to have a new conversation with a new friend and see what ensues.

15 CONCLUSION

In your journey of reading this book you've traveled along with me through lighthearted subjects and others that were deadly serious. I wanted to inform you and share ideas. I hope I've helped you envision new possibilities across a range of categories from food and comfort to wealth and economy and even your own personal economy. But, more than that, I wanted to provoke you. Upon reading this book, I hope you become activated.

If you faced a medical emergency you'd want immediate help. And, if your home were threatened by wildfire or worse, actually on fire, you'd likewise want immediate help. Providing remedies to crises and solving problems is important to each of us. If you faced these situations you'd wish that someone was activated, somebody able and willing to help you.

But, often times in our own neighborhoods and in the broader global village there are persistent problems that don't constitute a crisis; there is no immediate fire; it may be getting close, but there's still time. We sometimes fall for the illusion that if things are far away, or invisible to us, then they don't much matter — that is, until they do. Remember Niemöller's poem, "First they came for …"?

Also, things happen gradually before they happen suddenly as we know from the day old bread theory. Your medical emergency and potential fire are not in isolation. They may be connected to mind, mouth, and muscle or an unarrested spark. They could also be connected to other things unknown, and perhaps unknowable.

The Featherless Crow

I returned to my home one afternoon and heard a ruckus in my backyard. Overhead there was a dark cloud. There must have literally been more than one hundred crows scattered in the trees overhead. I gave up counting at eighty since I was getting bombed with branches as crows diligently pecked them free.

The crows were furious and I was confused and a little fearful, too. Bird images from Alfred Hitchcock's horror film *The Birds*, flashed in my mind. After retreating to the safe confines of my home I looked through the window to better understand what was happening. There appeared to be fledgling crows on the ground. Whether they were nudged to move ahead in life ahead of time or a wind gust gave them premature flight, the tiny featherless chicks had no hope of flying. There they sat, prey for the curious neighborhood cats and raccoons, save for the murder of crows overhead that would continue to stand guard.

Over the next several days there were a few periodic ventures into the yard to redirect the misguided crows from hazards such as stairwells. For a little while, I lost site of the crows and feared the worst. Then, I saw some unusual activity in the far corner of my yard.

Little, newly feathered crows were hopping up the bank onto progressively higher rocks, and then jumping off the ledge at the top, honing their flying skills as gravity played its part. It was quite a treasure to see the featherless birds mature and eventually turn their clunky sky jumps into masterful flight.

What I witnessed was that practice makes perfect, not training. Like baby crows, we need to practice those things we wish to become proficient in. Training alone seldom provides the opportunity for mastery. Imagine a baby crow sitting through the crow equivalent of flight instruction. Without the hours spent flying (or trying) the real world lessons would come slowly, if ever.

I've never looked at crows the same since my featherless crow experience. Those birds sparked me to action. Saving baby crows was not on my list for that day or any day, but I did it.

As Edward Deming said, "The most important things cannot be measured." It's true, many things fall into that category. But, it doesn't mean they are not important, or that there is nothing to be done. Saving a couple of strange birds seemed like the right (and unmeasurable) thing to do.

> ## "I will prepare and some day my chance will come."
>
> *Abraham Lincoln*
> *16th President*
> *of the United States,*
> *(1809–1865)*

Imagine that people were freed to pursue the ideas in this book. Participatory Budgeting frees up some portion of public budget in many cities as discussed briefly in the Chapter 5: Wealth & Economy. But, imagine if other private capital got behind these ideas. Imagine we stopped amassing trillions of dollars to sit idle and instead diverted it toward supporting promising ideas that advanced the human condition: new national parks, a Make Meaning Department, public-private partnerships in an Innovation Clearinghouse, new services and gadgets to make life more comfortable or people more prosperous.

Ideas that can reduce discord and bring peace and harmony have billions of allies at the ready. Perhaps you have one of these ideas.

You might not readily see these allies because the network-for-human-progress social media site has not yet been established. But, be certain there is a figurative equivalent to the Pots and Pans Revolution going on somewhere in the world right now; perhaps it's at your antipodal point.

You are like the juror in the modern day jury box. You've been exposed now to many things. Things you cannot possibly unthink. The thoughts you've already began to have in your Velcro-like mind are forming little hooks; they have already started clinging to other ideas, information, and possibilities.

You stand ready to connect what you see, read, hear and discuss with others, to what you've already stored in your mind. You are like the baby crow, practicing.

Maybe you are an Abraham Lincoln in the making. Did you know he is the only U.S. president to hold a patent? He was a avid learner, building his brain like the Velcro that was not yet invented. Lincoln probably had encounters with the natural inspiration, the Burdock plant, since it was native to Illinois and Kentucky, two places where Lincoln lived and spent time outdoors. Perhaps he too, thought of a nature inspired fastener system, but didn't pursue it. Maybe he was too busy practicing law?

One of the books Lincoln read was Benjamin Franklin's autobiography. Lincoln later used information from Franklin's Farmers' Almanac to challenge the credibility of an eyewitness during his most notable criminal trial. Based on the evidence, Lincolns' client was acquitted.

You see, Abraham Lincoln practiced. Like a baby fledgling crow, he practiced. There was no law school for Lincoln; he taught himself. He built a brain like Velcro, like you're doing right now.

But, even if you're not a Abraham Lincoln, that's okay (we all are by the way). But, ok, so you don't believe it. It's fine; instead, you can empower one, ten, or one hundred other Lincolns.

Remember there are many flavors of entrepreneurship, the impossipreneur is but one. Lincoln's patent was never commercialized.

Good ideas will persevere because the world finds it hard to resist an idea whose time has come. Much technology has changed since Lincoln's day. But, many of our social systems are stuck in time. Lincoln worked tirelessly to put slavery in the museum. But, slavery has merely shifted forms, close to home and far away.

Whether you are the next entrepreneur, impossipreneur or you spark another one to action, it doesn't matter.

As I said in the introduction, your imagination is a powerful force. I'm glad that you're on the team.

I wrote this book to build allies, perhaps you are one. Do you want to make the Innovation Clearinghouse real? Me, too. Do you wish every nation's government provided its citizens with a Make Meaning Department? Me, too.

There is too much for me to do alone. I hope you'll join me on a hopeful journey through tomorrow.

Welcome to the team.

Thank you for reading my book. I hope you found it entertaining and informative. I also hope it sparked some insight for you to follow. Perhaps you'll be the next [name of famous entrepreneur here].

Good luck and remember if you enjoyed this book, please write a positive review and tell all of your friends in person and on social media. And, if you didn't like it, please tell nobody and wake up from this terrible dream you're having. ☺

END NOTES

INTRODUCTION
[1] Radiolab podcast on emergence
http://www.radiolab.org/story/91500-emergence/

CHAPTER 1
[1] History of the Java Jacket
http://www.javajacket.com/about-java-jacket/history/

CHAPTER 2
[1] Learn more at the National Parks Timeline from THE
NATIONAL PARKS, American's Best Idea, a Film by Ken
Burns.
http://www.pbs.org/nationalparks/history/timeline/

[2] Listing of acreage as of December 31, 2011 Land
Resource Division, National Park Service.
http://www.nps.gov/parkhistory/online_books/haines1/ie
e3a.htm

[3] National Park Service,
http://www.nps.gov/aboutus/index.htm

[4] Hermann Sprengel (1865) "III. Researches on the
vacuum,"Journal of the Chemical Society, vol. 18, pages 9-
21.
https://en.wikipedia.org/wiki/Sprengel_pump

[5] Leap of faith: Dick Fosbury on how a new jump style
changed his sport forever
http://www.olympic.org/news/leap-of-faith-dick-fosbury-
on-how-a-new-jump-style-changed-his-sport-
forever/229513

[6] Drug schedules from the United States Drug

Enforcement Administration (DEA)
http://www.dea.gov/druginfo/ds.shtml

[7] A Look at U.S. Marijuana laws
http://www.cnn.com/interactive/2014/01/politics/map-
marijuana/

[8] See Initiative Rights by State
http://www.citizensincharge.org/states

[9] 1,000-2,000 New Marijuana Jobs In Colorado
http://mjbizdaily.com/1000-2000-new-cannabis-jobs-in-
colorado/

[10] Erin Brockovich Lends Support To Water Quality
Fight In Gardena
http://www.dailybreeze.com/environment-and-
nature/20150430/erin-brockovich-lends-support-to-water-
quality-fight-in-gardena

[11] Lyon, France, 20 March 2015 – The International
Agency for Research on Cancer (IARC), the specialized
cancer agency of the World Health Organization, has
assessed the carcinogenicity of five organophosphate
pesticides.
http://www.iarc.fr/en/media-
centre/iarcnews/pdf/MonographVolume112.pdf

[12] The vast majority of Americans feel they have a right to
know what is in their food.
http://www.justlabelit.org/right-to-know-center/polls-
surveys/

[13] These are the U.S. Representatives who voted to ban
GMO labeling and deny your right to know what you're
eating.

http://www.naturalnews.com/050525_DARK_Act_GMO
_labeling_House_of_Representatives.html

[14] Glyphosate damages DNA, says World Health
Organisation expert
http://www.gmwatch.org/news/latest-news/16302-
glyphosate-damages-dna-says-world-health-organisation-
expert

[15] Pope Francis' Encyclical letter Laudato si'
http://w2.vatican.va/content/francesco/en/encyclicals/do
cuments/papa-francesco_20150524_enciclica-laudato-
si.html

[16] Hack the Commute
A Joint Effort by the City of Seattle and Partners
http://hackthecommute.seattle.gov/#sthash.YE4DCgBf.t3
8to5cX.dpbs

App that helps people in wheelchairs plan travel routes wins
first place at civic hackathon
http://www.geekwire.com/2015/app-that-helps-people-in-
wheelchairs-plan-travel-routes-wins-first-place-at-civic-
hackathon/

[17] The Wright Brothers & The Invention of the Aerial
Age". Smithsonian Institution.
http://airandspace.si.edu/exhibitions/wright-
brothers/online/

[18] Child Labor Public Education Project
http://www.continuetolearn.uiowa.edu/laborctr/child_lab
or/about/us_history.html

CHAPTER 3
[1] Hispanic Consumers Are The 'Foundation' For Beauty

Category Sales
http://www.nielsen.com/us/en/insights/news/2015/hispa
nic-consumers-are-the-foundation-for-beauty-category-
sales.html

[2] Brazil's Booming Beauty Industry Births A New
Billionaire
http://www.forbes.com/sites/andersonantunes/2014/01/
16/brazils-booming-beauty-industry-births-a-new-
billionaire/

[3] 'The Lipstick Effect': Women Spend More On Beauty
Products During Recessions, Study Says
http://www.huffingtonpost.com/2012/06/19/the-lipstick-
effect-women-beauty-recessions_n_1606298.html

[4] Over-50s women spent most on make-up
http://www.telegraph.co.uk/news/celebritynews/1153593
1/Over-50s-women-spent-most-on-make-up.html

[5] Because You're Worth it - The Story Behind the
Legendary Phrase
http://www.lorealparisusa.com/en/about-loreal-
paris/because-yo

[6] 2013 Plastic Surgery Statistics Report
http://www.plasticsurgery.org/Documents/news-
resources/statistics/2013-statistics/plastic-surgery-statistics-
full-report-2013.pdf

[7] Reading Our Lips: The History of Lipstick Regulation in
Western Seats of Power, page 13
http://dash.harvard.edu/bitstream/handle/1/10018966/Sc
haffer06.pdf?sequence=1

[8] Oral Health: Warning signs You should Never Ignore

http://www.webmd.com/oral-health/america-asks-
12/oral-warnings?page=1

[9] Mining the Mouth's Many Microbes
The oral cavity contains several distinct and dynamic
microbial communities, and some of these commensals may
seed the body's other microbiomes.
http://www.the-
scientist.com/?articles.view/articleNo/40281/title/Mining-
the-Mouth-s-Many-Microbes/

[10] Human Oral Microbiome Database
The goal of creating the Human Oral Microbiome Database
(HOMD) is to provide the scientific community with
comprehensive information on the approximately 700
prokaryote species that are present in the human oral
cavity.
http://www.homd.org/

[11] Heart Cells And Brain Cells Have The Same DNA
Sequence, But Aren't Actually The Same
http://www.medicaldaily.com/pulse/heart-cells-and-brain-
cells-have-same-dna-sequence-arent-actually-same-322788
Contains Great Video on the Subject of Epigenetics

[12] What is the epigenome? National Human Genome
Research Institute
https://www.genome.gov/27532724

[13] Nature vs. Nurture: An Introduction to Epigenetics
https://www.illumina.com/company/video-
hub/YPN9mAJIaKw.html

[14] Ibid.

[15] Heart Cells And Brain Cells Have The Same DNA

Sequence, But Aren't Actually The Same
http://www.medicaldaily.com/pulse/heart-cells-and-brain-cells-have-same-dna-sequence-arent-actually-same-322788
Contains Great Video on the Subject of Epigenetics

[16] 'Epigenetic' concepts offer new approach to degenerative disease
http://www.eurekalert.org/pub_releases/2010-04/osu-co042810.php

[17] Genetic techniques have role in future of dental care
http://www.sciencedaily.com/releases/2014/03/140306095115.htm

[18] The Giant Sequoia
Olson, Gregory (2013-11-12). The Experience Design BLUEPRINT: Recipes for Creating Happier Customers and Healthier Organizations (Kindle Locations 744-745). Gregory James Olson. Kindle Edition. ISBN 9781503072251

[19] The Giant Sequoia
Asa Gray, Longeuity of Trees, quoted in Rodney Sydes Ellsworth, The Giant Sequoia, pp. 94-95; American Journal of Science, 2nd series, vol. 17, 1846-1870, reprint 1857 (pp. 440-443).

[20] Scientific Papers of Asa Gray: Selected by Charles Sprague Sargent
Asa Gray Charles Sprague Sargent - January 1, 1889
Houghton, Mifflin and Company, 1889

CHAPTER 4

[1] Mental Model
https://en.wikipedia.org/wiki/Mental_model

[2] Fatal police shootings in 2015 approaching 400 nationwide
http://www.washingtonpost.com/national/fatal-police-shootings-in-2015-approaching-400-nationwide/2015/05/30/d322256a-058e-11e5-a428-c984eb077d4e_story.html

[3] Helen Keller Facts
McGinnity, B.L., Seymour-Ford, J. and Andries, K.J. (2004) Helen Keller. Perkins History Museum, Perkins School for the Blind, Watertown, MA.

CHAPTER 5

[1] 2015's States Most & Least Dependent on the Federal Government
http://wallethub.com/edu/states-most-least-dependent-on-the-federal-government/2700/

[2] Bankrupt Cities, Municipalities List and Map
http://www.governing.com/gov-data/municipal-cities-counties-bankruptcies-and-defaults.html

[3] After losing parents, 6-year-old embarks on smile mission
http://www.cbsnews.com/news/after-losing-parents-6-year-old-embarks-on-mission/

[4] What is the Empathy Museum?
We are launching the world's first Empathy Museum, an experiential adventure space for stepping into the shoes of other people and looking at the world through their eyes. It will be an international travelling exhibition – starting out in London – and will exist online too. The Empathy Museum is dedicated to developing the skill of empathising and creating a global revolution of human relationships.
http://www.empathymuseum.com

[5] The Importance of Young Firms for Economic Growth
http://www.kauffman.org/what-we-
do/resources/entrepreneurship-policy-digest/the-
importance-of-young-firms-for-economic-growth

[6] A Brief History: Universal Health Care Efforts in the US
http://www.pnhp.org/facts/a-brief-history-universal-
health-care-efforts-in-the-us

[7] What a Hundred Million Calls to 311 Reveal About New
York
http://www.wired.com/2010/11/ff_311_new_york/

[8] BklynShare: Check out an Expert & Borrow a Skill! A
new approach to knowledge sharing
https://www.newschallenge.org/challenge/libraries/evaluat
ion/bklynshare-check-out-an-expert-borrow-a-skill-a-new-
approach-to-knowledge-sharing

[9] The History of Coworking
http://www.tiki-toki.com/timeline/entry/156192/The-
History-Of-Coworking-Presented-By-
Deskmag/#vars!panel=1506142!

[10] Parisians have their say on city's first €20m
'participatory budget'
http://www.theguardian.com/cities/2014/oct/08/parisian
s-have-say-city-first-20m-participatory-budget

[11] The case against the 'gig economy'
http://fortune.com/2015/07/30/freelance-vs-full-time-
employees/

[12] The Experience Design Blueprint: Recipes for Creating
Happier Customers and Healthier Organizations, Chapter

14: The World of Work has Changed
Olson, Gregory (2013-11-12). (Kindle Locations 3826-3827). Gregory James Olson. Kindle Edition.
Page 307 Hardcopy

[13] Founding of Médecins Sans Frontières
http://www.doctorswithoutborders.org/founding-msf

[14] MSF Treats People Wounded by Macedonian Border Troops
http://www.doctorswithoutborders.org/article/msf-treats-people-wounded-macedonian-border-troops

[15] Hundreds of refugees breach Macedonia border
http://www.aljazeera.com/news/2015/08/thousands-stuck-macedonian-border-bottleneck-greece-150822081819406.html

[16] A-To-Z Guide Of The World's "Without Borders" Groups
http://matadornetwork.com/change/a-to-z-guide-of-the-worlds-without-borders-groups/

[17] Engineers Without Borders International - Field of Action
http://www.ewb-international.org/fields-of-action/

[18] Rural village gets water infrastructure upgrade
http://www.ee.co.za/article/rural-village-get-water-infrastructure-upgrade.html

[19] I-5 Skagit River Bridge reopens with new permanent replacement
http://www.kirotv.com/news/news/i-5-skagit-river-bridge-permanent-span-set-go/nZxWB/

[20] Governor proclaims state of emergency due to I-5 bridge collapse on Skagit River
http://www.governor.wa.gov/news-media/governor-proclaims-state-emergency-due-i-5-bridge-collapse-skagit-river

[21] The idea of Oikocredit
http://www.oikocredit.coop/about-us/history/the-idea-of-oikocredit

[22] Workers Without Borders: The Philippines
http://www.bbc.co.uk/programmes/p02rsx98

[23] The Philippine Overseas Employment Administration (POEA)
http://www.ofwguide.com/directory_poea.php

[24] "I Already Bought You"
Abuse and Exploitation of Female Migrant Domestic Workers in the United Arab Emirates
https://www.hrw.org/report/2014/10/22/i-already-bought-you/abuse-and-exploitation-female-migrant-domestic-workers-united

[25] Introduction to International Labour Standards
http://www.ilo.org/global/standards/introduction-to-international-labour-standards/lang--en/index.htm

[26] 5 Effects of Poverty
http://borgenproject.org/5-effects-poverty/

[27] Unconditional Basic Income: Two pilots in Madhya Pradesh
http://www.guystanding.com/files/documents/Basic_Income_Pilots_in_India_note_for_inaugural.pdf

[28] SWITZERLAND: Government reacts negatively to UBI proposal
http://www.basicincome.org/news/2014/08/switerland-government-reacts-negatively-to-ubi-proposal/

[29] Basic Income: transforming lives in rural India
https://www.opendemocracy.net/openindia/stuart-weir/basic-income-transforming-lives-in-rural-india

[30] Alaska Permanent Fund Corporation Frequently Asked Questions
http://www.iser.uaa.alaska.edu/Publications/bien_xiii_ak_pfd_lessons.pdf

[31] The Alaska Permanent Fund Dividend: A Case Study in Implementation of a Basic Income Guarantee, page 10 and 11
http://www.iser.uaa.alaska.edu/Publications/bien_xiii_ak_pfd_lessons.pdf

CHAPTER 6

[1] Introduction to the Death Penalty: Early Death Penalty Laws
http://www.deathpenaltyinfo.org/part-i-history-death-penalty#early

[2] Penal Transportation - Origin and Implementation
https://en.wikipedia.org/wiki/Penal_transportation

[3] The Capricornian - The Latest Wonder. Page 14
http://trove.nla.gov.au/ndp/del/article/65763678

[4] 3.1 Human Body Chemical Composition
http://www.foresight.org/Nanomedicine/Ch03_1.html

[5] Quarks to Quasors: How Does Observing Particles

Influence Their Behavior?
http://www.fromquarkstoquasars.com/how-does-observing-particles-influence-their-behavior/

[6] Emerging Nations Embrace Internet Mobile Technology: Cell Phone Nearly Ubiquitous in Many Countries
http://www.pewglobal.org/2014/02/13/emerging-nations-embrace-internet-mobile-technology/

[7] Cashless Africa: Kenya's smash success with mobile money
http://www.cnbc.com/2013/11/11/cashless-africa-kenyas-smash-success-with-mobile-money.html

[8] December 15, 2010 in person interview with CEO Michael Kollins, CEO of World Bicycle Relief
http://www.worldbicyclerelief.com

[9] Inattentional blindnesson Scholarpedia
http://www.scholarpedia.org/article/Inattentional_blindness

[10] Motolight Motorcycle Lights "I see." Said the blind man!"
http://www.motolight.com/page/481485610

[11] Hövding the world's first airbag for cyclist: How it Works
http://www.hovding.com/how_hovding_works

[12] International Transport Forum: Road Safety Annual Report 2014
http://temis.documentation.developpement-durable.gouv.fr/documents/Temis/0069/Temis-0069702/19103_2014.pdf

[13] 8 Things You May Not Know About Jonas Salk and the Polio Vaccine
http://www.history.com/news/8-things-you-may-not-know-about-jonas-salk-and-the-polio-vaccine

[14] All Our Patent Are Belong to You
http://www.teslamotors.com/blog/all-our-patent-are-belong-you

[15] The main benefits of Platooning
http://www.scania.com/Images/The_main_benefits_of_Platooning_tcm40-396489.pdf

[16] The Safety Truck Could Revolutionize Road Safety
http://global.samsungtomorrow.com/the-safety-truck-could-revolutionize-road-safety/

[17] Jaguar Land Rover Develops Transparent Pillar And 'Follow-Me' Ghost Car Navigation Research
http://newsroom.jaguarlandrover.com/en-in/jlr-corp/news/2014/12/jlr_virtual_urban_windscreen_151212/

CHAPTER 7

[1] Full Quote from fictional character in The Hobbit
"If more of us valued food and cheer and song above hoarded gold, it would be a merrier world. But, sad or merry, I must leave it now. Farewell." Thorin Oakenshield
https://en.wikipedia.org/wiki/Thorin_Oakenshield

[2] Last Week Tonight with John Oliver: Food Waste (HBO)
https://www.youtube.com/watch?v=i8xwLWb0lLY

[3] Taste the Waste Documentary
http://tastethewaste.com/info/film

[4] World Resources Report
http://www.wri.org/tags/world-resources-report

[5] Food wastage footprint: Impacts on natural resources
http://www.fao.org/docrep/018/i3347e/i3347e.pdf

[6] Ibid.

[7] FoodSharing.de Overall Statistics
https://foodsharing.de/statistik

[8] RipeNear.Me Mission, Goals, and Aims.
http://www.ripenear.me/about-ripenearme

CHAPTER 8

[1] The Global Refugee Crisis: A Conspiracy of Neglect
http://static.guim.co.uk/ni/1434356535972/The-Global-Refugee-Crisis-a.pdf

[2] Malala Yousafzai
https://en.wikipedia.org/wiki/Malala_Yousafzai

[3] The Nobel Peace Prize for 2014
http://www.nobelprize.org/nobel_prizes/peace/laureates/2014/press.html

[4] Mark Zuckerberg Facebook update August 27 at 1:33pm
"We just passed an important milestone. For the first time ever, one billion people used Facebook in a single day.
On Monday, 1 in 7 people on Earth used Facebook to connect with their friends and family.
When we talk about our financials, we use average numbers, but this is different. This was the first time we reached this milestone, and it's just the beginning of connecting the whole world.

I'm so proud of our community for the progress we've made. Our community stands for giving every person a voice, for promoting understanding and for including everyone in the opportunities of our modern world.
A more open and connected world is a better world. It brings stronger relationships with those you love, a stronger economy with more opportunities, and a stronger society that reflects all of our values.
Thank you for being part of our community and for everything you've done to help us reach this milestone. I'm looking forward to seeing what we accomplish together."

https://www.facebook.com/zuck/posts/10102329188394581?pnref=story

http://www.zdnet.com/article/facebook-hits-1-billion-users-in-one-day/

[5] Internet.org is a Facebook-led initiative bringing together technology leaders, nonprofits and local communities to connect the two thirds of the world that doesn't have internet access.
https://internet.org/about

[6] Universal Declaration of Human Rights
http://www.un.org/en/documents/udhr/

[7] Orange to soothe the Reykjavik streets?
http://www.icenews.is/2009/01/25/orange-to-soothe-the-reykjavik-streets/

[8] Iceland's Rainbow Revolution
http://grapevine.is/mag/articles/2009/02/06/icelands-rainbow-revolution/

[9] Global Nonviolent Action Database

Icelanders overthrow top power holders responsible for economic crisis (Kitchenware Revolution), 2008-9
http://nvdatabase.swarthmore.edu/content/icelanders-overthrow-top-power-holders-responsible-economic-crisis-kitchenware-revolution-20

[10] Access to European Union Law
2.2. The financial crisis and major causes of failure of the Icelandic banks (15)
http://eur-lex.europa.eu/legal-content/EN/TXT/?uri=uriserv:OJ.L_.2014.144.01.0169.01.ENG

[11] Interview with Sherron Watkins
http://www.fraud-magazine.com/article.aspx?id=583

[12] A Look Back at the Enron Case
https://www.fbi.gov/news/stories/2006/december

[13] Lay and Skilling's day of reckoning
Enron ex-CEO and founder convicted on fraud and conspiracy charges; sentencing slated for September.
http://money.cnn.com/2006/05/25/news/newsmakers/enron_verdict/index.htm

[14] The Pentagon Papers. 1971 YEAR IN REVIEW
http://www.upi.com/Archives/Audio/Events-of-1971/The-Pentagon-Papers

[15] Daniel Ellsberg
https://en.wikipedia.org/wiki/Daniel_Ellsberg

[16] Whistle Blower's Legal Victory Seen As Supporting Industry Scientists Who Criticize Their Employers
http://www.the-scientist.com/?articles.view/articleNo/28348/title/Whistle-

Blower-s-Legal-Victory-Seen-As-Supporting-Industry-Scientists-Who-Criticize-Their-Employers/

[17] Whistleblower Protection Enhancement Act Of 2012: R E P O R T Of The Committee On Homeland Security And Governmental Affairs United States Senate
http://www.gpo.gov/fdsys/pkg/CRPT-112srpt155/pdf/CRPT-112srpt155.pdf

[18] UN Special Rapporteur for Freedom of Expression Delivers Strong Guidance on Whistleblower
http://whistleblower.org/blog/104714-un-special-rapporteur-freedom-expression-delivers-strong-guidance-whistleblower
Full Report: Promotion and protection of the right to freedom of opinion and expression
http://www.un.org/ga/search/view_doc.asp?symbol=A%2F70%2F361&Submit=Search&Lang=E

[19] 5 Famous Whistleblowers Who Shaped History,
3. Bradley Manning
http://mic.com/articles/49867/5-famous-whistleblowers-who-shaped-history

[20] Collateral Murder - Wikileaks - Iraq
https://www.youtube.com/watch?v=5rXPrfnU3G0&feature=youtu.be

[21] List of Whistleblowers
https://en.wikipedia.org/wiki/List_of_whistleblowers

[22] Edward Snowden
https://en.wikipedia.org/wiki/Edward_Snowden

[23] The Right Livelihoood Award
http://www.rightlivelihood.org/snowden.html

[24] U.S. Nonprofit Stands Up for United Nations Whistleblowers
http://nonprofitquarterly.org/2015/09/17/u-s-nonprofit-stands-up-for-united-nations-whistleblowers/

[25] Pope Francis' Encyclical letter Laudato si'
VII. A Variety Of Opinions - 61.
V. Civic And Political Love - 231.
I. Environmental, Economic And Social Ecology - 139.
II. The Globalization Of The Technocratic Paradigm- 112.
III. The Mystery Of The Universe - 78.
http://w2.vatican.va/content/francesco/en/encyclicals/documents/papa-francesco_20150524_enciclica-laudato-si.html

[26] What is the Holocaust by Bullets?
http://www.yahadinunum.org/background/?lang=en

[27] Holocaust investigator on parallel between Nazis and ISIS
http://www.cbsnews.com/news/holocaust-investigator-on-parallel-between-nazis-and-isis/

[28] Together In One
http://www.yahadinunum.org/mission/why-yahad-in-unum

[29] MAP OF EXECUTION SITES -Investigated by Yahad - In Unum
http://yahadmap.org/#map/

[30] George Orwell. Politics and the English Language
http://www.orwell.ru/library/essays/politics/english/e_polit

[31] Hans and Ola Rosling: How not to be ignorant about the world

https://www.ted.com/talks/hans_and_ola_rosling_how_n
ot_to_be_ignorant_about_the_world/transcript?language=
en

[32] You Need to Know: What Do Natural, Local and
Organic Mean?
http://www.huffingtonpost.com/eve-turow/you-need-to-
know-what-food-regulation_b_5596171.html

[33] Neuroplasticity
https://en.wikipedia.org/wiki/Neuroplasticity

[34] A New Response to Crisis? Jón Ólafsson on the Case
of Iceland
http://berkeleyjournal.org/2014/10/a-new-response-to-
crisis-jon-olafsson-on-the-case-of-iceland/

[35] John F. Kennedy "Man on the Moon" speech.
Excerpt from an Address Before a Joint Session of
Congress, 25 May 1961
http://www.jfklibrary.org/Asset-
Viewer/xzw1gaeeTES6khED14P1Iw.aspx

[36] Murray, Charles; Cox, Catherine Bly (1989). Apollo:
The Race to the Moon. New York: Simon & Schuster.
ISBN 0-671-61101-1

[37] Allen, Bob (ed.). "NASA Langley Research Center's
Contributions to the Apollo Program". Langley Research
Center. NASA. Retrieved August 1, 2013. NASA Langley
Research Center's Contributions to the Apollo Program
http://www.nasa.gov/centers/langley/news/factsheets/Ap
ollo.html

CHAPTER 9
[1] Massive deforestation risks turning Somalia into desert

http://archive.cosmosmagazine.com/features/massive-deforestation-risks-turning-somalia-desert/

[2] Report of the World Commission on Environment and Development. Our Common future, Brundtland report. United Nations 1987
http://www.are.admin.ch/themen/nachhaltig/00266/0054 0/00542/index.html?lang=en

[3] A Call for the National Implementation of the Basic Income Brant (BIG) in Namibia
http://www.bignam.org/Publications/Press_release_July_2 015.pdf

[4] Relief through cas. Impac assessment of the ermergcy cash gran tin Namibia.
http://www.bignam.org/Publications/Relief_through_cash _Impact_assessment_of_the_emergency_cash_grant_in_N amibia.pdf

[5] Hippocratic Oath
https://en.wikipedia.org/wiki/Hippocratic_Oath

[6] Divine Chocolate on Food Forum
http://www.foodforum.org.uk/ffiles/Divine_Chocolate-Inn+Mat+Man+Pro+Con-KS3+KS4.shtml

[7] Frequently Asked Questions
http://www.divinechocolate.com/us/about-us/frequently-asked-questions#Farmers

[8] Ghanian Farmers in Control
http://www.oikocreditnorthwest.org/l/library/download/ urn:uuid:1f172249-26fb-469a-9770-3f2a1ed65772/in-focus-sheet-kuapa-kokoo-english.pdf

[9] The Dark Side of Chocolate, A Film by Miki Mistrati &
U. Roberto Romano
http://www.thedarksideofchocolate.org/

[10] Martin Niemöller: "First they came for the
socialists...."
http://www.ushmm.org/wlc/en/article.php?ModuleId=10
007392

[11] New circular economy package takes shape
http://www.euractiv.com/sections/sustainable-dev/new-
circular-economy-package-takes-shape-319006

[12] About Zero Waste Europe
http://www.zerowasteeurope.eu/about/

[13] The Cradle to Cradle Products Innovation Institute
http://www.c2ccertified.org/about

The Cradle to Cradle Certified™ Product Standard
http://www.c2ccertified.org/get-certified/product-
certification

[14] Pilot Study: Impacts of the Cradle to Cradle Certified
Products Program: PUMA Company Narrative
http://s3.amazonaws.com/c2c-
website/resources/Final_PUMA_narrative_formatted.pdf

Puma Bring Me Back Program
http://about.puma.com/en/sustainability/products/bring-
me-back-program

[15] America's Forum | Astronaut Ron Garan discusses
working on the International Space Station
http://www.newsmaxtv.com/vod/Americas-Forum--
Astronaut-Ron-Garan-discusses-working-on-the-

International-Space-
Station/vid/x5eDVwczrG9Az3Jph5iNRBuw2H9M-
qYC/#ooid=x5eDVwczrG9Az3Jph5iNRBuw2H9M-qYC

[16] Tidal giants - the world's five biggest tidal power plants
http://www.power-technology.com/features/featuretidal-
giants---the-worlds-five-biggest-tidal-power-plants-
4211218/

[17] Catching Waves and Turning Them Into Electricity
http://www.nytimes.com/2015/04/23/business/energy-
environment/catching-waves-and-turning-them-into-
electricity.html?ref=topics

[18] How drinking water pipes can also deliver electric
power
http://www.pbs.org/newshour/bb/drinking-water-pipes-
can-also-deliver-electric-power/

[19] Floating turbines could harness the awesome power of
the tides
http://www.theecologist.org/blogs_and_comments/Blogs
/2985189/floating_turbines_could_harness_the_awesome_
power_of_the_tides.html

[20] Relocating Newtok
https://orionmagazine.org/article/relocating-newtok/

[21] Living on the Brink: What will happen to the residents
of the sinking Ghoramara island in the Sunderbans
http://indianexpress.com/article/india/india-others/living-
on-the-brink-what-will-happen-to-the-residents-of-the-
sinking-ghoramara-island-in-the-
sunderbans/#sthash.dmulCPot.dpuf

[22] COMPACT OF FREE ASSOCIATION: Agreement

between the UNITED STATES OF AMERICA and the
MARSHALL ISLANDS
http://www.state.gov/documents/organization/173999.pd
f

[23] Environment Agency: 7,000 properties to be lost to sea
http://www.bbc.com/news/science-environment-
30627285

[24] Massive deforestation risks turning Somalia into desert
http://archive.cosmosmagazine.com/features/massive-
deforestation-risks-turning-somalia-desert/

[25] U.S. Environmental Protection Agency (EPA).
Washington, DC. "Protecting Water Quality from Urban
Runoff." Document No. EPA 841-F-03-003. February
2003.

[26] Green Cities: Good Health. Mental Health & Function
https://depts.washington.edu/hhwb/Thm_Mental.html

http://www3.epa.gov/npdes/pubs/nps_urban-
facts_final.pdf

[27] Sea organ on the new marine parade of the Zadar
peninsula.
http://www.publicspace.org/en/projects/d078-morske-
orgulje/prize:2006

[28] Nikola Bašić, author of the Zadar Sea Organ at the
Croatian World Network (CROWN)
http://www.croatia.org/crown/articles/9359/1/nikola-
baiae-author-of-the-zadar-sea-organ.html

[29] Five Things You Don't Know About Zadar
http://landlopers.com/2013/07/14/zadar

[30] Captured Sounds of the Sea Organ of Zadar
http://www.free-stock-music.com/the-sea-organ-of-zadar.html

[31] Energy Research and Development Division
Final Project Report: Assessment Of Piezoelectric
Materials For Roadway Energy Harvesting
http://www.energy.ca.gov/2013publications/CEC-500-2013-007/CEC-500-2013-007.pdf

[32] What are the main sources of carbon dioxide
emissions?
http://whatsyourimpact.org/greenhouse-gases/carbon-dioxide-sources

[33] Biomass from algae
http://www.renewableenergyfocus.com/view/931/biomass-from-algae/

[34] A Look Back at the U.S. Department of Energy's
Aquatic Species Program: Biodiesel from Algae
http://www.nrel.gov/docs/legosti/fy98/24190.pdf

[35] Renewable biological systems for alternative sustainable
energy production (FAO Agricultural Services Bulletin -
128). Chapter 1 - Biological energy production
http://www.fao.org/docrep/w7241e/w7241e05.htm#1.2.1

[36] Emerging solar harvesting technology could turn
windows into power sources
http://ceramics.org/ceramic-tech-today/emerging-solar-harvesting-technology-could-turn-windows-into-power-sources

CHAPTER 10
[1] The Marihuana Tax Act of 1937 Transcripts of

Congressional Hearings. Additional statement of H. J. Anslinger, commissioner of narcotics
http://www.druglibrary.org/schaffer/hemp/taxact/t10a.htm

[2] Comprehensive Drug Abuse Prevention and Control Act of 1970
http://www.gpo.gov/fdsys/pkg/STATUTE-84/pdf/STATUTE-84-Pg1236.pdf

[3] Hemp Facts
http://www.naihc.org/hemp_information/hemp_facts.html

[4] Did the Government Give Industrial Hemp a Pass to Clean Up Radiation in the States?
http://www.nationofchange.org/did-government-give-industrial-hemp-pass-clean-radiation-states-1392388637

[5] Video Of Senator Ron Wyden Introducing Bill To Lift The Federal Ban On Industrial Hemp.
https://youtu.be/oPEF9eFqBwY

[6] Neuralyzer from the 1997 movie, Men in Black
https://en.wikipedia.org/wiki/Neuralyzer

[7] US Bus Drivers Still Coping With Bathroom Access Issues
http://www.ibtimes.com/us-bus-drivers-still-coping-bathroom-access-issues-1831252

[8] Too few bathroom breaks drove bus drivers to adult diapers
http://crosscut.com/2014/11/king-county-bus-drivers-depends/

[9] Eminent domain
https://en.wikipedia.org/wiki/Eminent_domain

[10] Murray, Constantine, City Council declare emergency, announce new investments to respond to homelessness
http://murray.seattle.gov/category/homelessness/#sthash.PCDzcKDw.dpuf

[11] Being Homeless in This City Will Get You a One-Way Bus Ticket out of Town
http://www.takepart.com/article/2014/09/08/being-homeless-city-will-get-you-one-way-bus-ticket-out-town

[12] A data visualisation studio and decision making space housed within the Data Science Institute
https://www.imperial.ac.uk/data-science/about-the-institute/facilities/kpmg-data-observatory-/

[13] Buckminster Fuller - World Game
https://bfi.org/about-fuller/big-ideas/world-game

CHAPTER 11
[1] How A Machine Learned To Spot Depression
http://www.npr.org/sections/money/2015/05/20/407978049/how-a-machine-learned-to-spot-depression

[2] Can Pets Sense Our Emotions
https://www.superhappypets.com/article_pets_sense_emotions.html

[3] If I had a magic phone
https://www.youtube.com/watch?v=jWtFeIw8MVM

[4] About Stool Tests
http://kidshealth.org/parent/general/sick/labtest8.html#

CHAPTER 12
[1] Majority of U.S. Employees Not Engaged Despite Gains in 2014
http://www.gallup.com/poll/181289/majority-employees-not-engaged-despite-gains-2014.aspx

CHAPTER 13

CHAPTER 14
[1] Examining the Mob Mentality
http://source.southuniversity.edu/examining-the-mob-mentality-31395.aspx#sthash.sXFngXc6.dpuf

[2] Antipodes Map
http://www.antipodesmap.com/

CHAPTER 15
[1] Lincoln's Patent
http://www.abrahamlincolnonline.org/lincoln/education/patent.htm

INDEX

ABOUT THE AUTHOR

Gregory J. Olson is the author of *The Experience Design Blueprint*, a book about designing better experiences and then making them come true. He founded strategy and design firm, Delightability, LLC. with the belief that if you delight customers, success will follow. A lifelong learner, his formal education includes a BSEE and MBA from Seattle University. Gregory also serves as a volunteer board member for Oikocredit Northwest, a support association for social investor and financial institution, Oikocredit International.

The Experience Design Blueprint

ISBN 9781503072251